rororo sprachen
Herausgegeben von
Ludwig Moos

Idioms sind der Schlüssel zur Sprache. Wer genügend Redewendungen beherrscht, hat viel vom Geist einer Sprache begriffen und kommt beim Sprechen nicht mehr so leicht in Verlegenheit. "Master your Idioms" bietet den Schlüssel zu den gebräuchlichsten englischen Redewendungen. Nach Schlüsselwörtern geordnet, werden rund tausend Idioms vorgestellt und mit deutschen Entsprechungen erklärt. Kurze Satzbeispiele verdeutlichen den Verwendungszusammenhang. In a word: put everything into the right words and you won't have to eat your words.

Ernest Pasakarnis, gebürtiger Amerikaner litauischer Herkunft, arbeitet nach Zeiten als Sprachlehrer und Redakteur in einem Schulbuchverlag inzwischen als Übersetzer und Autor nichtschulischer Sprachbücher. In der Reihe rororo sprachen liegen ferner von ihm vor: "Grammar Questions from A to Z" (8359) und der moderne Vokabeltrainer "How Words Work" (8426).

Ernest Pasakarnis

Master your Idioms

Der Schlüssel zu den englischen Redewendungen

Zeichnungen Mathias Hütter

ro
ro
ro

Rowohlt

Originalausgabe
Veröffentlicht im Rowohlt Taschenbuch Verlag GmbH,
Reinbek bei Hamburg, November 1988
Copyright © 1988 by Rowohlt Taschenbuch Verlag GmbH,
Reinbek bei Hamburg
Umschlagtypographie Peter Wippermann
(Umschlagbild Gerd Huss)
Satz Times und Helvetica (Linotron 202)
Gesamtherstellung Clausen & Bosse, Leck
Printed in Germany
1280-ISBN 3 499 18491 5

Inhalt

Vorwort

Was ist das eigentlich, ein Idiom? Nun, es ist ein Mehrwortausdruck
oder ein Satz, dessen Bedeutung im allgemeinen nicht aus der
Übersetzung der einzelnen Wörter hervorgeht. Anders gesagt, ein
Idiom ist eine feste sprachliche Verbindung, die etwas anderes
bedeutet als das, was die einzelnen Wörter aussagen.
Master Your Idioms ist der Schlüssel zu einem Vorrat an tausend
Redewendungen. Im Grunde jedoch ist die ganze englische Sprache
idiomatisch. Wenn Sie mit Hilfe dieses Buches erst einmal Zugang zur
Welt der Idioms gefunden haben, werden Sie feststellen, daß man
diese überall antrifft – sei es in der Sachliteratur, einem Roman, einer
Zeitung, einem Gespräch, einem persönlichen Brief oder in einer
Illustrierten. *Master Your Idioms* legt besonderen Wert auf die in der
täglichen Umgangssprache gebräuchlichen Redewendungen. Es ist
für jeden geeignet, der ein lebendiges Englisch sprechen möchte.
Einige Redewendungen kennen Sie vielleicht bereits. Um so besser.
Manche werden öfter angewandt als andere. Es gibt Bücher, in denen
versucht wird, so viele Redewendungen wie möglich aufzuführen.
Das kann einen Leser jedoch überfordern. Ich möchte die allgemein
gebräuchlichen Redewendungen hervorheben. Sie können sofort
damit beginnen, sie in Ihrer Unterhaltung mit englischsprachigen
Personen anzuwenden. Versuchen Sie es! Es wird Ihnen gefallen, und
Ihren Gesprächspartnern auch. Der mündliche und schriftliche
Gebrauch der Redewendungen wird Ihrem ganzen Sprachstil mehr
Sicherheit verleihen, Sie werden sich der Sprache und ihres Aufbaus
insgesamt bewußter.
Die Redewendungen sind alphabetisch unter Schlüsselwörtern
sortiert, zum Beispiel CRY, DAY, EARLY, GET, HAT, HEAD,
NOTHING... Am besten schlagen Sie das Buch einfach irgendwo
auf, und beginnen Sie zu lesen. Ich habe Beispielsätze gegeben, die
Ihnen verdeutlichen, wie die Redewendungen in Gesprächen des

Alltags benutzt werden. Manche dieser Beispiele sind traurig, manche fröhlich und manche, wie ich hoffe, auch witzig.

Ich wünsche mir, daß Sie mit diesem Buch viel Spaß haben. Wenn ja, aber auch, wenn Sie Einwände haben, lassen Sie mich das bitte wissen. Sie können mir über den Verlag schreiben. Ich bekomme gern Post von meinen Lesern, und ich antworte auch immer.

Mehr bleibt nicht zu sagen. Nehmen wir den Schlüssel zur Hand, öffnen wir die Tür, gehen wir hinein und machen wir uns mit der faszinierenden Welt der englischen Redewendungen bekannt.

Master your Idioms

A

ABC

as easy as ABC
kinderleicht
George always thought that learning idioms was difficult. But he's found out that it's not true. *Master Your Idioms* makes the learning of idioms as easy as ABC.

ABOUT

be up and about again
wieder auf den Beinen sein
After being in the hospital for three months with a broken leg, I am really glad to be up and about again. It's a great feeling.

ACE

have an ace in the hole
noch einen Trumpf in der Hand haben
The big advertising agency was positive that it would get the contract from the large computer company. What it didn't know was that the little advertising agency had an ace in the hole. And as things turned out, it was the little advertising agency that got the big contract from the large computer company.

ACID

the acid test
Feuerprobe
They say that the acid test of a good friendship is the first seven years.

ACT

be caught in the act
auf frischer Tat ertappt werden
The burglar had just opened the safe and had started to take out the jewels and the money when the man of the house walked into the room with a gun in his hand. The burglar was caught in the act.

put on an act
Theater spielen
Gerry says that he feels old and tired and not much use to anyone. But it's not true. He's just putting on an act.

ADD

add insult to injury
eine Angelegenheit noch verschlimmern, eine Sache noch schlimmer machen
After yelling and screaming at her at the top of his voice, he added insult to injury by telling her that he didn't love her.

add to the confusion
die Verwirrung noch größer machen
The situation was bad enough as it was. But Paul added to the confusion by saying that he wasn't going to tell anyone where he had been the night before and what he had done.

AGE

act your age
sei kein Kindskopf!
"You're a grown man, Henry," said his wife. "So stop crying like a little baby and act your age!"

be of age
volljährig, mündig sein
My children are of age now and they can do whatever they want.

come of age
volljährig, mündig werden
My son came of age last week. It was his eighteenth birthday.

AGENDA

be on the agenda
auf der Tagesordnung stehen, auf dem Programm stehen
What's on the agenda for today? I'm going to do the shopping. Then I'm going to make lunch. And then in the evening I'm going to go and see a new film at the local theatre.

AIR

be up in the air about something
über etwas aufgeregt sein, außer sich sein, aus dem Häuschen sein
Martina was up in the air about the fact that her little brother had spilled ketchup on her new white dress at the breakfast table.

be walking on air
im siebten Himmel sein
Helen has been walking on air ever since Gene asked her to go to the school dance with him.

build castles in the air
Luftschlösser bauen
They say that neurotics build castles in the air. Psychotics live in them.
And that psychiatrists collect the rent for them.

AKIMBO

with arms akimbo
die Arme in die Seiten gestemmt
Someone once told me that if a person gets up and then stands with
arms akimbo, he is then subconsciously ready for a fight.

ALIVE

alive and kicking
gesund und munter
He wrote a short letter to his sister to let her know that he was alive
and kicking.

look alive
beeilen Sie sich!
"Look alive," said the sergeant to the soldiers that were slow in getting up from their beds in the morning.

ALL

for all I know
soviel ich weiß
Nobody knows where Ernest is these days. For all I know, he might
even be in Outer Mongolia.

do it all the same
es trotzdem tun
We told him that it would be crazy to spend so much money on a new
camera. But do you think he listened to us? No, he went out and did it
all the same.

be all the same to someone
einem gleich, egal sein
Would you like to see a new film in town or watch TV or read a book or
play tennis with me? Oh, it's all the same to me.

be not all there
eine Schraube locker haben, nicht ganz bei Trost sein
After Mike broke up with his girlfriend after three years, he became a
changed person. His friends could tell that he wasn't all there. Love is
blind but after a while he could see again.

when all is said and done
letzten Endes
When all is said and done it is you who has to make the final decision
whether you want to become a doctor or not.

ANGLE

a new angle
ein neuer Gesichtspunkt
We thought that we had considered all the angles. But John came up
with a new angle as to how to solve the problem. And we did.

know all the angles
alle Kniffe kennen
Alan is the bright boy of the company. He knows all the angles when it
comes to selling computers to customers who like to say no.

APPLE

be the apple of someone's eye
jemandes Augapfel sein
He is really a romantic man, because he keeps telling his wife that she
is the apple of his eye. And you know what? She loves it.

be the apple of someone's eye

in apple-pie order
in Butter, in bester Ordnung
My wife and I are healthy. Our children are healthy. I have a good job.
My house is paid for. We are happy. Everything is in apple-pie order.

upset someone's applecart
jemandes Pläne durchkreuzen, zunichte machen
Losing my job really upset my applecart. My wife and children and I
wanted to fly to the Bahamas for a holiday this summer.

ASK

there is no harm in asking
fragen kostet nichts
"Do you think that he would sell me his car? I just love it, Mary."
"There is no harm in asking. Why not go over to his place this evening
and find out what he has to say, Paul."

she is asking for it
sie fordert es heraus
She's been late ten times this month. The boss is really angry. She'll probably lose her job. After all, she's been asking for it.

ask for trouble
das Unglück herausfordern
If you go around criticizing the boss all the time and telling him how to do his job, you are asking for trouble.

AXE

get the axe
rausfliegen, rausgeschmissen werden
Well, it finally happened to George. He criticized his boss all the time. And he told him how to do his job. Well, George got the axe this morning. Now he's looking for a new job.

B

BAG

be left holding the bag
der Dumme sein
My boss told me that he wanted me to explain the matter to the president of the company. Before I could say no, the president walked in and demanded an explanation from me. My boss had left the office in the meantime. I was left holding the bag.

be left holding the bag

be nothing but a bag of bones
nur noch Haut und Knochen sein
"Your should eat more and smoke less," I said to Waltraud. "Just take a look in the mirror. You're nothing but a bag of bones."

have something in the bag
etwas so gut wie sicher haben
I'm very happy today because I'm fairly sure that I've got that job in the bag.

BALL

play ball
mitmachen
The detective was a man of courage. He wouldn't play ball with the gangsters even when they said that they might kidnap his son.

16

be on the ball
auf Draht sein, auf Zack sein
When it comes to making a dollar, that boy is really on the ball.

get the ball rolling
eine Sache in Gang bringen
"Come on, men," said the foreman, "let's get the ball rolling. We haven't got all day."

have a ball
sich königlich amüsieren
I really had a ball at last night's party.

have a lot on the ball
viel auf dem Kasten haben
You might not like him but you have to admit that he really has a lot on the ball when it comes to computers and software.

keep the ball rolling
das Gespräch/eine Sache in Gang halten
The meeting was coming along fine. Although it was lunchtime, he didn't want to stop the meeting. The ideas were flowing freely and he wanted to keep the ball rolling.

BARK

his bark is worse than his bite
Hunde, die bellen, beißen nicht
He is a very kind and gentle and understanding person. But sometimes you'd never know it because his bark is often worse than his bite.

bark up the wrong tree
auf falscher Fährte sein, an die falsche Adresse gekommen sein
Listen, Alphonse! If you think I'm going to lend you all that money and that's the only reason you came here, well, you're barking up the wrong tree.

BAT

go to bat for someone
für jemanden eine Lanze brechen
All the employees in the office love their manager, because they all
know that he will go to bat for them when things get rough.

without batting an eye
ohne mit der Wimper zu zucken
He is a mean boss. He can fire people on the spot without batting an
eye. Sometimes he even puts on a happy face.

BEAN

not know beans about something
keinen blassen Schimmer von etwas haben
He failed his exam because he didn't know beans about the history of
France.

spill the beans
etwas ausplappern, die Katze aus dem Sack lassen
"All right," said the gangster, "I want you men to find the guy who
spilled the beans about our plan to rob the bank."

BEAUTY

beauty is only skin deep
der Schein trügt
They say that beauty is only skin deep but ugliness is to the bone.

that's the beauty of it
das ist eben das Schöne daran
This computer is simple, easy to use, inexpensive and weighs very
little. That's the beauty of it.

BEGGAR

beggars can't be choosers
einem geschenkten Gaul schaut man nicht ins Maul
"This is not exactly the job that I wanted to have," said the man that was unemployed, "but then again, beggars can't be choosers."

BELT

hit below the belt
unter der Gürtellinie treffen; unfair handeln, kämpfen
You really have to watch out when you're discussing business matters with him, because he really knows how to hit below the belt.

tighten one's belt
den Gürtel enger schnallen
Now that father has lost his job all of us in the family are going to have to tighten our belts.

belt someone
jemanden verhauen
If you don't shut your mouth right away, I'm going to belt you one.

BIRD

a bird in the hand is worth two in the bush
besser ein Spatz in der Hand als eine Taube auf dem Dach
"Mike, I've just won a thousand dollars playing roulette here in Las Vegas. I'm going to try again. I'm going to place a thousand-dollar bet."
"Don't, Ernest! You know what they say?"
"What do they say?"
"A bird in the hand is worth two in the bush."

a little bird told me
der kleine Finger hat es mir gesagt
"How did you know that roses are my favourite flowers?" "A little bird told me."

kill two birds with one stone
zwei Fliegen mit einer Klappe schlagen
Would you like to come with me to Niagara Falls? I have some business there that I have to take care of. And afterwards we could take in some of the sights. We could kill two birds with one stone.

BITTER

take the bitter with the sweet
Angenehmes und Unangenehmes gleicherweise hinnehmen
Life isn't all peaches and cream or just a bowl of cherries. Oftentimes you have to take the bitter with the sweet. That's the way it is.

BLUE

like a bolt out of the blue
wie ein Blitz aus heiterem Himmel
When my old friend Mike showed up at my front door after all those years, it was like a bolt out of the blue.

have the blues
in gedrückter Stimmung sein
There's the story about a man who had the blues because he had no shoes. But then upon the street he met a man who had no feet.

sing the blues
Trübsal blasen
John's wife left him. Then the bank took his house and car away. Yesterday he lost his job. And so today he is singing the blues.

once in a blue moon
alle Jubeljahre
Yes, I do drink champagne but only once in a blue moon.

BOIL

boil down to this
auf folgendes hinauslaufen
Roslyn, what it boils down to is that they don't really want you to come
to the party, but they don't know how to tell you without hurting your
feelings.

at the boiling point
auf dem Siedepunkt
Frank's temper was at the boiling point when he found out that he had
missed his plane for New York.

at the boiling point

BONE

a bone of contention
ein Zankapfel
That island in the Atlantic has often been a bone of contention between those two countries.

feel something in one's bones
eine Vorahnung von etwas haben
I don't know why but I just know something wonderful is going to happen today. I can feel it in my bones.

have a bone to pick with someone
mit jemandem ein Hühnchen zu rupfen haben
Robert has a bone to pick with Helen, because she forgot to water his plants while he was away. After all, she had promised.

work one's fingers to the bone for someone
sich für jemanden abschinden
Their mother worked her fingers to the bone for her children, but they never ever said a word of thanks.

BOTTOM

from the bottom of my heart
aus tiefstem Herzen
I'd like to thank you from the bottom of my heart for all the kind and wonderful things you've done for me.

hit bottom
auf Grund geraten, den tiefsten Stand erreichen
They say that it's not really a bad thing when a person hits bottom, because then there is only one place to go and that is up.

bet one's bottom dollar on something
sein letztes Geld auf etwas setzen, Gift darauf nehmen
You can bet your bottom dollar, George, on the fact that you and your girlfriend are through.

BREAD

know which side one's bread is buttered on
wissen, wo etwas zu holen ist; sich auf seinen eigenen Vorteil verstehen
You don't have to tell Mike and Olga that they have excellent positions with the company. They're not going to quit good jobs like that, because they know very well which side their bread is buttered on.

BREWERY

smell like a brewery
eine Fahne haben
Alan must have had one cocktail too many for lunch this afternoon. He smells like a brewery.

BROKE

be broke
pleite sein
I don't have a penny to my name. I am completely broke.

go broke
pleite gehen
At one time GB stood for Great Britain. Then GB stood for going broke. And now GB stands for getting better.

go for broke
aufs Ganze gehen
Mr. Blackstone had already lost a lot of money on business deals. He was almost penniless. But then he gave it one more try. He risked all the money he had left on one final business deal. He went for broke. And you know what? Fortune smiled upon him.

BUCKET

a drop in the bucket
ein Tropfen auf den heißen Stein
Of course I can help them out by giving them money. But they really need big help. My help would be just a drop in the bucket.

come down in buckets
in Strömen gießen
Every time I forget to take my umbrella with me it always starts to come down in buckets.

kick the bucket
ins Gras beißen
Do you remember Gino the old wine drinker? Well, after 40 years of wine drinking, he finally kicked the bucket.

BULL'S-EYE

score a bull's-eye
ins Schwarze treffen
Daniel scored a bull's-eye with his first advertising campaign for a large soap company. The company increased its sales by 22 %.

BUT

ifs, ands, and buts
Wenn und Aber
I just don't think Horst is ever going to write that novel he has been talking about. He's always coming up with too many ifs, ands, and buts.

no ifs, ands, or buts
keine Ausrede, ohne Wenn und Aber
Just do as I tell you, Manuela. Clean up your room right now. And, please! No ifs, ands, or buts!

BYGONES

let bygones be bygones
die Vergangenheit ruhen lassen
I know, Uli, that you and I have had our arguments and our quarrels.
And I know that a lot of unpleasant things have happened in the past.
But let's forget about them. Come on, let's let bygones be bygones.

C

CAKE

a piece of cake
kinderleicht
I passed the examination with no problems at all. It was a piece of
cake. After all, I had studied for it a long time.

that takes the cake
nun schlägt's dreizehn, das ist doch die Höhe
I've seen and heard a lot of things in my lifetime. But what you did this
morning... Well, all I can say is that that really takes the cake!

sell like hot cakes
wie warme Semmeln weggehen
These new personal computers are really popular with the end users.
Although they're not exactly inexpensive, they're selling like hot
cakes.

want to have one's cake and eat it too
auf zwei Hochzeiten tanzen wollen, alle Vorteile haben wollen
Michael bought himself a big brand-new car so that he could take his
family on a nice summer holiday. But cars and vacations cost a lot of
money. His wife told him that he couldn't have his cake and eat it
too.

CALL

close call
knappes Entkommen
The car almost hit him on the street. But he was able to jump out of the way just in time. Nevertheless, it was a close call.

call it a day
Feierabend machen
After writing two chapters for his new book, George Scanlan said to his wife, "Honey, I'm ready to call it a day."

call the shots
das große Wort führen
Mr. Carruthers is the boss around here and that is the only reason he gets to call the shots.

CANDLE

not hold a candle to someone
jemandem nicht das Wasser reichen können
Algernon Blackstone writes good mystery stories for young people, but he doesn't hold a candle to George Scanlan. George's stories are absolutely fantastic and wonderful.

burn the candle at both ends
mit seiner Gesundheit aasen, seine Kräfte unnütz verschwenden
Helga works hard by day and by night. She has two jobs. She needs the money. On weekends she stays up until the wee small hours of the morning drinking and dancing. Her friends say that she is burning the candle at both ends. But Helga just says, "Yes, it's true. But my candle gives such a lovely light."

CANOE

paddle one's own canoe
sich aus eigener Kraft durchs Leben schlagen
If there's one thing their father taught them it was how to paddle your own canoe. He knew he wouldn't always be around to take care of his sons; so he taught them the art of survival.

paddle one's own canoe

CARD

lay one's cards on the table
mit offenen Karten spielen
The nice thing about him as a person and as a friend is that he always lays his cards on the table. He never says one thing and then does another.

throw in the cards
die Flinte ins Korn werfen
I really admire Lance, because if he doesn't succeed at first, he tries
and tries again. He is not a man that throws in the cards at the first sign
of difficulty or trouble.

CARE

be free from care
sorgenfrei sein
People are wrong when they think that a life free from care will make
them happy. It's often the challenges and the trials and the tests of life
that make people strong and happy.

I couldn't care less
das ist mir schnurzegal
"Helen, did you know that Robert is coming over to see you this afternoon? He's crazy about you." "I couldn't care less. I've got another
boyfriend."

I don't care
es ist mir gleich
I don't care what people say about me. I always say, "Everything that
you have heard about me is true."

care for someone
jemanden mögen oder gern haben
If you care for me, Martina, then stay just the way you are.

what do I care?
was kümmert's mich?
It might be snowing outside. The wolves may be howling at the door.
But what do I care? I've got my small house to keep me warm.

CART

put the cart before the horse
das Pferd beim Schwanz aufzäumen
She's always doing things in the wrong order. She's the kind of person that turns on the washing machine and then puts in the dirty clothes. She's always putting the cart before the horse.

CARTE BLANCHE

give someone carte blanche
jemandem einen Freibrief ausstellen
"Mr. Jones, we are giving you carte blanche. You can deal with the matter in any way, shape or form that you consider to be proper. The success of the negotiations lies in your hands," said the president of the company to his best manager.

CAST

the die is cast
die Würfel sind gefallen
"There's nothing you can do now, Ernest. You've made your decision. There's no going back. The die is cast."

cast a spell on someone
jemanden behexen, bezaubern
Lars is in love with Gudrun and none of us knows why. We think that Gudrun must have cast a spell on him.

cast one's lot in with someone
mit jemandem gemeinsame Sache machen
When the revolution started, it was surprising how many people cast their lot in with the revolutionaries.

cast pearls before swine
Perlen vor die Säue werfen
I really don't understand why you continue to do all those things for
them. They don't understand it and above all they don't appreciate it.
It's like casting pearls before swine.

CATCH

there's a catch to it
die Sache hat einen Haken
The house is beautiful and it's in a good location. And it's also very
inexpensive. George doesn't know why. His wife says to him, "Honey, there must be a catch to it somewhere."

catch on
Anklang finden, Schule machen
It's amazing how fast microwave ovens have caught on with the house-
wives of America.

catch someone's eye
jemandem ins Auge fallen
A beautiful diamond ring caught my eye yesterday and so I decided to
buy it for my wife's birthday. She loved it.

CAUTION

throw caution to the wind
kühn vorgehen, handeln
George threw caution to the wind by walking into his boss's office and
saying that he wanted more money or else he would quit his job there
and then.

catch someone's eye

CEILING

hit the ceiling
an die Decke gehen, hochgehen
It's almost impossible to live with Brian. You just say one little wrong word and he hits the ceiling. As a matter of fact, Brian spends most of his time up there.

CENT

be not worth a red cent
keinen roten Heller wert sein
That contract in your hand, Mike, is just a piece of paper. It's not worth a red cent. It's worthless. They really fooled you when you signed that contract.

put one's two cents' worth in
seinen Senf dazugeben
This is a discussion between Helga and me, Gerry. I don't want you putting your two cents' worth in all the time.

CHANCE

chances are
man darf wohl annehmen
You can try calling him at this hour, but chances are that you won't get any answer. He's usually out at this time.

jump at the chance
die Gelegenheit beim Schopf packen
When that big bank in New York offered me a position in the credit department, I jumped at the chance right away.

not stand a chance of
keine Aussicht haben auf
I am sad and lonely and unhappy, because I know that I don't stand a chance of ever winning her love.

take a chance
sein Glück versuchen
If you never take a chance on something new or adventurous or risky, then you'll never get anywhere in life.

take one's chances
es darauf ankommen lassen
You're crazy to go to Alaska. You're not going to find any gold in those hills. "I'll take my chances, Frank," he said to me.

CHASE

a wild-goose chase
ein vergebliches Suchen
They said that I could find the item I was looking for in that store near the post office. But it wasn't true. I went to 16 stores this afternoon but couldn't find the thing I was looking for. It was just a wild-goose chase and nothing more.

CHEAP

dirt cheap
spottbillig
I hardly paid anything for my used car. It was dirt cheap.

CHEW

bite off more than one can chew
sich zuviel vornehmen oder zumuten, sich überfordern
I am sure that all of you out there in the audience know that there were times in my life when I bit off more than I could chew.

CHIP

be a chip off the old block
ganz der Vater sein
What can you expect from Gerry but good and wonderful things. After all, he's a chip off the old block.

have a chip on one's shoulder
die beleidigte Leberwurst spielen
Don't pay any attention to Sven this morning. He's in a bad mood. I think he always wakes up with a chip on his shoulders on Monday mornings.

chip in fifty dollars for
fünfzig Dollar beisteuern zu
I'll tell you what I'm going to do. I'm going to chip in 50 dollars for
your birthday party.

CLASH

the colours clash
die Farben beißen sich
The nice thing about money is that its colour never clashes with the
colour of the clothes you're wearing.

CLOUD

every cloud has a silver lining
es gibt nichts Schlechtes auf der Welt, was nicht etwas Gutes
nach sich zieht
At the time he thought that losing his wife to another man was the end
of the world. But not too long after their break-up, he met the love of
his life and they lived happily ever after. It just goes to show that every
cloud has a silver lining.

have one's head in the clouds
in Gedanken vertieft sein, in höheren Regionen schweben
Professor Winterbottom is our new mathematics teacher. He always
has his head in the clouds. He's probably thinking about new theo-
rems and formulas all the time.

cloud the issue
eine Streitfrage verdunkeln
Politicians are experts when it comes to clouding the issue.

have one's head in the clouds

COAST

the coast is clear
die Luft ist rein
"Okay, men, you can come out now," said their friend. "The police have gone. The coast is clear now."

COLD

be left out in the cold
ignoriert werden
My wife and I once went to a party where I was the only man. I couldn't believe it but I was left out in the cold by all the women.

leave someone out in the cold
jemanden vernachlässigen, stiefmütterlich behandeln
My girlfriend is so interested in her new job that lately she's been leaving me out in the cold.

my blood runs cold
mich gruselt es; das Blut erstarrt mir in den Adern
My blood runs cold every time I think about what could have happened on the highway last week if I hadn't stopped the car in time.

get cold feet
eine Heidenangst bekommen, kalte Füße kriegen
At first he was all for the plan but now he's getting cold feet.

give someone the cold shoulder
jemandem die kalte Schulter zeigen
She gave him the cold shoulder when he asked her to dance.

leave someone cold
jemanden kaltlassen
French perfume and Russian caviar leave me cold.

COME

easy come, easy go
wie gewonnen, so zerronnen
After he had won a million dollars at the roulette tables of Las Vegas in the morning, he lost it all the next afternoon. The gambler said, "Well, easy come, easy go."

first come, first served
wer zuerst kommt, mahlt zuerst
I was in a department store this afternoon and I wanted them to save a nice winter coat for me, but the assistant said that he was sorry he couldn't do that. It was a case of first come, first served.

come to naught
ins Wasser fallen, zu Wasser werden
When I lost my job last April, my plans for a nice summer holiday on Bermuda came to naught.

come true
sich erfüllen, wahr werden
Dreams usually come true in fairy tales but rarely in real life.

have it coming to one
es verdienen
I'm glad that the workers staged a strike. The management had it coming to them for a long time now.

where do I come in?
wo bleibe ich? wo bleiben meine Interessen?
"That's a very good plan and I like it," one of the men said to the boss, "but I'd like to know where I come in." "Oh, I'm sorry, Joe, I forgot all about you."

COOK

too many cooks spoil the broth
viele Köche verderben den Brei
We're going to ruin this project if we try to work in all our ideas and plans at once. Too many cooks spoil the broth and that is why we are going to have to decide upon only one plan.

his goose is cooked
er ist erledigt, ruiniert
The teacher found out which boy had written the words on the blackboard. "Johnny's goose is cooked now," said his friends.

cook up a story
eine Geschichte aushecken
You'd better cook up a good story if you don't want your wife to hit you over the head with a frying pan when you go home tonight.

what's cooking?
was gibt's? was ist los?
"What's cooking, Fred?" "Nothing much. We're just sitting around watching a little TV. That's all. Maybe later."

COOL

as cool as a cucumber
die Ruhe selber
He is always as cool as a cucumber in front of a TV camera.

keep cool
kaltes Blut bewahren
The best thing to do in a moment of crisis is to keep cool.

CORNER

the four corners of the earth
die entferntesten Winkel der Erde
Ernest is such a romantic. He always says things like, "Darling, I would travel to the four corners of the earth to be where you are."

the four corners of the earth

be just around the corner
vor der Tür stehen
It's sad now but happy days are just around the corner.

cut corners
die Ausgaben einschränken
Our company is always cutting corners, but the thing is that they do it in the wrong places. Some people never learn.

drive someone into a corner
jemanden in die Enge treiben
Don't try to drive him into a corner, because he can become as angry as a raging elephant if you do.

CRAM

cram for an exam
für eine Prüfung pauken, büffeln
I haven't opened a single book for my history class this semester. I'm going to cram for the next history exam this coming weekend.

cram something down a person's throat
eintrichtern, jemandem etwas einhämmern
The one thing that I don't like about Michael is that he is always trying to cram his political views down my throat.

CRY

be a far cry from
etwas ganz anderes sein als, weit entfernt sein von
A Volkswagen is a far cry from a Rolls Royce.

it's no use crying over spilt milk
vorbei ist vorbei, da nützt kein Jammern und Klagen
I know you paid a small fortune for that vase from the Ming dynasty. So you dropped it and now it's broken. Hundreds of pieces are lying on the floor. But it's no use crying over spilt milk. All your tears aren't going to put it back together again.

cry wolf
blinden Alarm schlagen
You've heard about the boy who cried wolf one time too many. One day the wolf really showed up and ate the boy and nobody came to rescue him because they didn't believe him any more.

it's a crying shame
es ist sehr schade, ein Jammer
Everybody in the office says that it's a crying shame that Bill didn't get a promotion but that Henry did. Bill is the better man for the job. But that's the way things go in life.

be a crybaby
ein Meckerer sein, ein Schreihals sein
"Okay, Bill, so you didn't get that promotion," said his wife, "but you don't have to be a crybaby about it."

CUP

that's not my cup of tea
das ist nicht mein Fall
I love Spain but bullfighting is not exactly my cup of tea.

CUT

cut someone short
jemandem ins Wort fallen, jemanden unterbrechen
I am a tall man but my wife is constantly cutting me short when we are having a conversation. I can hardly get a word in edgewise.

cut someone to the quick
jemanden tief verletzen
Uli's words cut Ernest to the quick. She told him that there was another man in her life.

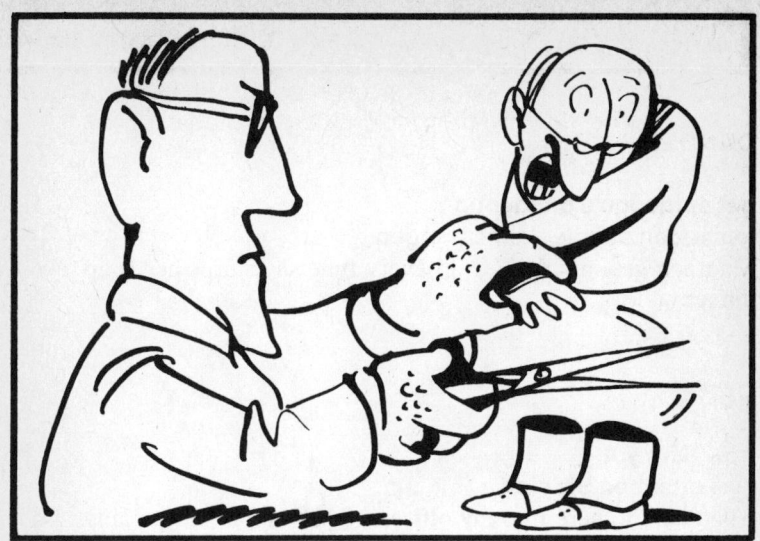
cut someone short

have one's work cut out for one
ein gutes Stück Arbeit vor sich haben
Professor Baltakis wants to write the best and most thorough and most interesting book on the Sanskrit language. Well, all we can say is that he has his work cut out for him.

be cut out for this work
für diese Arbeit wie geschaffen sein
He is quiet and mysterious. He speaks several languages. He loves his country. He is a brave man. He wants to be a secret agent. Yes, it's true: he is cut out for that kind of work.

D

DANDER

get someone's dander up
jemanden auf die Palme bringen
Maureen gets my dander up every time she slurps her soup at the dinner table.

DARE

how dare you
was erlauben Sie sich
You come in here into my office and call me all those names. And none of what you say is true. How dare you, James!

dare someone to do something
jemanden herausfordern, etwas zu tun
The pupils dared the new boy in class to light a fire in the teacher's wastepaper basket at lunchtime.

be a daredevil
ein Wagehals sein
He isn't afraid of any danger. Why, I've seen him jump from one tall building to another. Boy, he is a real daredevil.

DARK

shot in the dark
ein Sprung ins Ungewisse
I really didn't have any idea what the name of the virus was. It was a difficult and important medical exam. My answer was a shot in the dark. But it was the right shot. And I passed my medical exam with flying colours.

grope in the dark
im Dunkeln tappen

As usual, the police in this town are groping in the dark. They have no idea who or why or when the crime was committed.

things look rather dark
die Aussichten sind trübe

Business is bad this time of year. Sales are down. The customers are few and far between. I know that things look rather dark right now. But things are sure to get better soon.

look on the dark side of things
schwarzsehen

Nicholas is a real pessimist. He says things like: "It's darkest before the dawn before it turns completely black." We have never been able to figure out why he always looks on the dark side of things in life.

DATE

have a blind date with someone
ein Stelldichein mit einer/einem Unbekannten haben

My friend Ernest is a good friend. He has a nice girlfriend. And his girlfriend has a friend that doesn't have a boyfriend. Ernest invited his girlfriend's friend and Ernest invited me, too. So, this evening I'm having a blind date with Ernest's girlfriend's friend. I'm looking forward to it.

keep up to date
auf dem laufenden bleiben

George always tries to keep up to date with the latest developments in the field of computer technology.

set a date
einen Termin festsetzen

Let's set a date for the party right now. How about next week on Friday at eight o'clock in the evening? Yes, that's fine with me.

have a blind date with someone

DAWN

at the crack of dawn
in aller Herrgottsfrühe
He is a good and disciplined writer. He gets up every day at the crack
of dawn to work on his new novel.

dawn on someone
jemandem dämmern
I was already at the airport when it dawned on me that I had forgotten
my passport.

DAY

forever and a day
auf immer und ewig
"Will you love me for a long, long time?" he asked his wife. And she
replied, "Yes, I'm going to love you forever and a day."

44

red-letter day
ein Glückstag, ein Freudentag
I got a new job today. And this afternoon I met the girl of my dreams. I also won a lot of money playing cards. Everything has been going wonderfully today. It's truly been a red-letter day.

her days are numbered
ihre Tage sind gezählt
Her days as the president of this perfume company are numbered.

make a day of it
sich einen vergnügten Tag machen
Our car broke down in a small village in the middle of France. The mechanic said that it would only be ready the next day. So, my wife and I decided to make a day of it by going on a nice picnic and taking a long walk in the countryside.

save money for a rainy day
sich einen Notgroschen zurücklegen
When my car broke down last week I was able to pay for the car repairs. Luckily, I had saved some money for a rainy day.

DEAD

as dead as a doornail
mausetot
When the car ran over the rabbit on the road, it was as dead as a doornail.

be dead set against something
absolut dagegen sein
You know that your father is dead set against you bringing all your friends over for a party this evening.

dead to the world
in tiefem Schlaf
He's had a very long and very hard day. He's up in his bedroom now – dead to the world.

come to a dead end
in eine Sackgasse geraten, auf ein totes Gleis geraten
The detective said, "I don't know where to go from here. I've done everything possible to help this investigation along, but somehow I've come to a dead end. And I have absolutely no idea what's going to happen next."

DEAL

it's a deal
abgemacht
"Look, Gerry, I'll give you my couch for your desk. What do you say to that?" "It's a deal! I've always liked your couch."

make a big deal out of something
eine große Geschichte aus etwas machen
It was an accident. He didn't mean to spill that glass of red wine on your new dress. It's not the end of the world, so please, Jane, don't go making a big deal out of it.

DELIVER

deliver the goods
die Erwartungen erfüllen, den Wünschen nachkommen
Alan promised his father that he would deliver the goods by studying hard for his exam and passing it with flying colours.

deliver goods
Waren liefern
Jack has a part-time job delivering goods for the local department store.

deliver the letters
Briefe zustellen
There's a little poem that people often write on the back of an envelope when they want the mailman to deliver the letters in a certain way:

Mailman:
De liver
De letter
De sooner
De better

DISCRETION

discretion is the better part of valour
Vorsicht ist die Mutter der Porzellankiste
When Ralph saw the five young, strong, angry men walking down the
street towards him, he turned around and quickly went the other way,
because he knew that discretion was the better part of valour.

DO

do or die
friß, Vogel, oder stirb
It was a case of finding a job quickly so that I could pay the rent and
feed my family or being thrown out onto the street. It was the old story
of do or die.

no sooner said than done
gesagt, getan
The nice thing that I like about Susan is that when you ask her to do
something or when she says that she'll do something, it's always a case
of no sooner said than done. She's great.

that will do
das genügt, reicht
This is not exactly the material I was looking for, but it will have to do
until the real thing comes along.

do all the talking
allein das Wort führen
When the police car stopped them, the husband quickly said to his
wife, "Let me do all the talking. I'll explain it to the policeman. Everything will be okay."

do business with someone
mit jemandem Geschäfte machen
"As always, Mr. Kostroff," said the managing director, "it has been a pleasure doing business with you."

do New York
New York besichtigen
You won't believe this but we really did do New York in one day.

do time
eine Strafe absitzen
We won't be seeing Mr. Valentino for quite a long while now, because he's going to be doing time for a bank robbery that didn't go so well.

DOG

let sleeping dogs lie
man soll schlafende Hunde nicht wecken
When you see Eleanor this evening, don't talk to her about her old boyfriend Frank. That would only cause problems and trouble for her emotionally. Just let sleeping dogs lie.

rain cats and dogs
Bindfäden regnen
You think that it's raining hard right now? You should see what the weather is like here on the island in October. That's when it rains cats and dogs and you can throw your umbrella away.

you can't teach an old dog new tricks
was Hänschen nicht lernt, lernt Hans nimmermehr
I know that a lot of people say and believe that you can't teach an old dog new tricks. But I believe that you are never too old to learn something new.

rain cats and dogs

DOUBLE

on the double
Im Laufschritt, schnellstens
When I was in the army all I ever heard from my sergeant was, "On the double." Now I'm out of the army and I'm married and I hear the same words from my wife now. You just can't win.

double-cross someone
jemanden hintergehen, ein falsches Spiel mit jemandem treiben
In the world of gangsters and criminals and spies, there is always someone double-crossing someone or somebody.

double talk
doppelzüngiges Gerede
Politicians are the great experts in the art of double talk. They say one thing but mean another; or they mean one thing and say another. All that double talk is so confusing.

double standard
mit zweierlei Maß messen
He says it's okay when he goes out drinking with the boys and stays up late. But it's not okay, he says, when she goes out with the girls drinking. He's applying a double standard.

DOUBT

be beyond the shadow of a doubt
ohne jeden Zweifel sein
The facts are perfectly clear. He loves her very much. It's beyond the shadow of a doubt.

be in doubt about something
im Zweifel sein über etwas
I was in doubt about whether I should put in a comma or leave it out. But then I remembered the words of my English teacher: "When in doubt, leave it out." And so I left the comma out.

cast doubt on something
etwas in Zweifel stellen
I just can't understand why that cynical man is always casting doubt on other people's good intentions. There is no reason to.

give someone the benefit of the doubt
jemandem trotz Zweifel Glauben schenken
"I really didn't take it from him," said the young boy to the policeman. The policeman wasn't sure whether the young boy was telling the truth or not. But he gave him the benefit of the doubt and let him go.

doubt someone's word
an jemandes Wort zweifeln
She trusts him completely. She doesn't doubt his word for a minute.

DOWN

down under
in Australien
We love living down under. It's nicer than southern California.

down to the present
bis in unsere Tage
Our company has been producing this quality soap and using the same old original formula right down to the present.

be down and out
elend dran sein, pleite sein
He lost absolutely everything in Melbourne: wife, money, car, his business. He was down and out down under.

down on one's luck
vom Glück verlassen sein
Although he's been down on his luck lately, he still remains optimistic. He takes it philosophically. "Into each life some rain must fall," he says.

let someone down
jemanden enttäuschen
"Don't let me down, Ernest," said Llewellyn to her son-in-law. "I want to see you and your wife back together again."

talk down to someone
herablassend mit jemandem reden
The nice thing about Gerald is that he never talks down to children or young people. He treats them with respect.

DOZEN

baker's dozen
dreizehn Stück
The grocer gave me a baker's dozen when I only wanted ten oranges. I guess he can't count so well on Mondays. I don't blame him.

by the dozen
dutzendweise
When I asked Mike why he always buys so much of one thing, he said, "Ernest, they're always cheaper by the dozen."

six of one, half dozen of the other
Jacke wie Hose
There is no difference between these two models really. They look a little bit different on the outside but inside they are technically the same. It's six of one, half dozen of the other.

DRAG

drag one's feet
schlurfen, das Arbeitstempo mit Absicht verlangsamen
The engineers in that department are dragging their feet on this important project and it's costing the company plenty.

drag someone through the mud
jemanden durch den Dreck ziehen
He is such a good and kind and wonderful man. And that's what makes it hard for me to understand why they are constantly dragging him through the mud. I guess they're just jealous.

an awful drag
eine schreckliche Plage
All I can say is that the party was an awful drag. Never again!

DRAIN

go down the drain
zunichte werden, ins Wasser fallen
The president didn't like my project idea. Well, there went three months of planning and working down the drain.

DRINK

soft drink
alkoholfreies Getränk

I don't drink wine or beer or vodka any more. I like drinking mineral water now, and an occasional soft drink. That's all.

buy someone a drink
jemandem einen ausgeben

"You look like you've just lost your best friend," said the man at the bar to me. "I have," I said. "Well, let me buy you a drink then and you can tell me all about it."

take to drink
zu trinken anfangen

It's the same old story. She left him for another man. And what did he do? Well, he took to drink and that was the ruin of him.

drink like a fish
saufen wie ein Loch

Waltraud used to drink like a fish but now she only drinks soft drinks.

drink oneself out of a job
eine Stelle wegen Trunksucht verlieren
It didn't take George Scanlan very long to drink himself out of a job last year. It took him three days and five bottles of gin.

drink someone under the table
jemanden unter den Tisch trinken
The men who were heavy drinkers were really surprised the next morning when they found out that Monica had drunk them all under the table. Because that's where they were: under the table.

drink to someone's health
jemandem zutrinken
"Here's to you and here's to me. And if we ever disagree, the heck with you, and here's to me," he said while drinking to Mary's health and emptying his glass of wine in one go.

DRIVE

drive someone out of his mind
jemanden verrückt machen
I had to leave and find another job. Working at the computer terminal all day was slowly but surely driving me out of my mind.

drive someone home
jemanden nach Hause fahren
You don't have to take the bus this evening. I have a car. I'll drive you home. It's no problem at all.

drive something home to someone
jemandem etwas klarmachen oder einbleuen
My girlfriend drove the fact home to me that she and I were through by introducing me to her new boyfriend at the party.

be driving at something
auf etwas hinauswollen, etwas im Sinn haben
I don't know what you are driving at but whatever it is I can tell you right now that I am not interested.

be the driving force behind something
bei etwas die Triebfeder sein
The driving force behind all his work is simply his love of money.

DROP

a drop in the bucket
ein Tropfen auf den heißen Stein
I know that money helps a lot of poor people in those countries but
still it's just a drop in the bucket compared to the amount of money
spent on guns and tanks and planes.

at the drop of a hat
bei dem geringsten Anlaß
You don't have to ask Ernie twice to tell a joke. He'll start telling
jokes at the drop of a hat. Some of them are funny, too.

drop in
auf einen Sprung vorbeikommen
A good friend of mine dropped in last night for a few minutes to say
hello and tell me how things were going in his life.

drop out
abbrechen, unterbrechen, austreten
Horst started to learn Spanish at a language school last year, but he
dropped out after a couple of months.

drop someone a line
jemandem ein paar Zeilen schreiben
The nice thing about Alan is that no matter how busy he is, he always
finds the time to drop me a line and tell me how things are in his life.
He is truly a good friend.

drop someone off
jemanden absetzen
I dropped Helen off at the corner of Bloor and Spadina.

drop someone a line

drop the subject
das Thema fallenlassen
She said, "Let's talk about money." And I said, "No, darling, let's
drop the subject and talk about something else."

DROWN

drown one's sorrow in drink
seinen Kummer im Alkohol ertränken
I have always liked that saying about the man who tried to drown his
sorrow in drink but he didn't succeed because his sorrows knew how to
swim.

drown out the noise
den Lärm übertönen
The people downstairs were having a party. It was loud. Mike drowned
out the noise by turning up the volume of his stereo.

DRUNK

be dead drunk
sternhagelblau sein
He was lying on the grass and saying, "Stop the world. I want to get off." Boy, he was really dead drunk.

get drunk
sich betrinken
Olga was very unhappy and she wanted to get drunk quickly. She did so by drinking a bottle of vodka in twenty minutes.

DUCK

take to something like a duck to water
bei etwas sofort in seinem Element sein
He took to computers and computer games like a duck to water.

be like water off a duck's back
nicht den geringsten Eindruck machen
They told him he was no good at his job. They warned him that they would fire him. They told him that they didn't like him personally. But to Frank it was all like water off a duck's back.

DUMPS

be down in the dumps
deprimiert, niedergeschlagen sein
They say that it is better to have tried and failed than not to have tried at all. Well, Ernest tried and failed. And that was why he was down in the dumps all week long.

DUTCH

give some Dutch courage
sich Mut antrinken
Mary saw a nice man sitting at the bar and she wanted to ask him to dance, because she saw that he wasn't going to ask her. So she gave herself some Dutch courage by drinking two glasses of red wine very quickly.

make it a Dutch treat
zusammen ausgehen, wobei jeder für sich selbst bezahlt
"I'd sure like to see that film tonight, Helen. How about being my guest?" "Well, Gene, I'd like to see that film too, but let's make it a Dutch treat, okay?" "Okay!"

go Dutch
getrennte Kasse machen
"Did Gene invite you to go see that film with him, Helen?" Martha asked her best friend. "Yes, he did but we went Dutch."

DYE

dyed-in-the-wool
waschecht
You can tell Walter all the bad news of the world. He will still say that things are getting better no matter what. He is indeed a dyed-in-the-wool optimist.

E

EAR

be all ears
ganz Ohr sein
Lucy is all ears when her boyfriend Charles starts telling her how wonderful he thinks she is.

be wet behind the ears
noch nicht trocken hinter den Ohren sein
Herbert thinks he knows everything about this business. But he's only been with our company for five months. In reality he is still wet behind the ears. He still has a lot to learn.

fall upon deaf ears
kein Gehör finden
If I've told Lucy once, I've told her a thousand times: she should change the oil in her car more often. But my advice fell upon deaf ears. Now her car needs a new motor.

have no ear for music
musikalisch unbegabt sein
I wish I could play the piano but I have no ear for music.

have one's ear to the ground
auf dem laufenden bleiben
If you want to know what is going on in this company, go and see Thomas. He's a man who knows almost everything because he always has his ear to the ground.

lend someone one's ear
jemandem Gehör schenken
When Percy wants someone to listen to him, he starts by quoting Shakespeare: Friends, Romans and countrymen, lend me your ears. His friends smile and listen to Percy.

play it by ear
je nach Lage der Dinge entscheiden, gefühlsmäßig handeln
I really would like to have that job with that company. And I just don't
know what to say or how to act at the interview. My father said to me
that I should simply play it by ear. That's always the best way. Just be
yourself and play it by ear.

prick up one's ears
die Ohren spitzen
I pricked up my ears when I heard the boss talking about a bonus.

turn a deaf ear to
taub sein gegen
My boss always turns a deaf ear to my requests for more money.

walls have ears
Wände haben Ohren
Be careful what you say when you go to that party tonight. The walls in
their house have ears. And big ones at that.

walls have ears

EARLY

be an early bird
ein Frühaufsteher sein
One of the reasons that he is a good writer is because he is also an early
bird. He's up before the sun is. He wakes up and goes straight to his
typewriter without even a cup of coffee.

the early bird catches the worm
Morgenstund' hat Gold im Mund
If you want to get a good seat at the open air concert, you have to get
there very early. You know what they say? The early bird catches the
worm.

EARTH

why on earth
warum in aller Welt
"Laura, I quit my job at the office this afternoon," said the husband to
his wife. "Now, why on earth did you do something crazy like that,
Robert?"

be down-to-earth
sachlich, unkompliziert, vernünftig sein
The nice thing about Aunt Laura is that she is a down-to-earth person.
She'll help you in a realistic way with her kind words.

come back down to earth
in die Wirklichkeit zurückkehren
I wanted to buy myself a Rolls-Royce but I quickly came back down to
earth when I took a look at how much money I earned.

move heaven and earth
Himmel und Erde in Bewegung setzen
When I was younger I had the feeling that I could move heaven and
earth to get things done. And I did get things done. But that was long
ago. Now I don't have the energy any more.

EASY

easier said than done
leichter gesagt als getan
All you have to do, Alvin, is to stop drinking, get another job, find a new place to live in, and then all your problems will take care of themselves. But I also know that that's easier said than done. It's going to take you a while.

take it easy
reg dich nicht auf, schon' dich
Okay, so you lost your job today. My advice is not to worry and not to hurry. Just take it easy and you'll soon see that things will get better.

get off easy
mit einem blauen Auge davonkommen
You're lucky that the policeman just told you to drive more slowly the next time instead of giving you a speeding ticket. All I can say is that you really got off easy this time.

live on easy street
gut situiert sein
Ever since Clyde won all that money in Las Vegas he has been living on easy street.

EAT

eat humble pie
zu Kreuze kriechen
They all said that I would never get anywhere in life because I was so lazy and foolish. Well, they're all eating humble pie now. I have my own company. And I have 300 people working for me.

eat one's heart out
sich vor Kummer verzehren
Listen, Lionel, there's no use in eating your heart out over Doris just because she left you for another man. Remember, there are a lot of other fish in the sea.

eat one's words
seine Worte zurücknehmen müssen
"Edward," my Aunt Kate said, "you'll never write a book in your life. You're just not intelligent enough." Well, I did write a book and my Aunt Kate had to eat her own words.

eat someone out of house and home
jemanden arm essen
We love our Uncle Tom but we are always afraid when he comes to visit us because he usually eats us out of house and home.

what's eating you
was ist dir über die Leber gelaufen?
I don't know what's eating you, Helen, but I hope it's not anything serious. Tell me about it. You'll feel better for sure.

EDGE

be on edge
nervös sein
He's been on edge ever since he stopped drinking red wine.

have an edge on someone
jemandem gerade noch voraus sein
Mike and James are both very good football players, but Mike definitely has the edge on James.

take the edge off something
etwas die Schärfe nehmen
After work George usually goes to a bar and has a few beers. "Ah," he says, sipping a glass of beer, "this sure takes the edge off a hard day's work."

not get a word in edgewise
nicht zu Worte kommen
My mother, my wife and my daughter were having a discussion about the world situation at the breakfast table. I wanted to say a few things myself but I couldn't get a word in edgewise.

EGG

a bad egg
ein schlechter Kerl
They say that Harry is a bad egg but I don't believe it.

put all one's eggs in one basket
alles auf eine Karte setzen
The president of the Nancy Sweetland Perfume Company made a wise decision in that she decided not to concentrate only on ladies' perfume but to diversify and also sell men's after shave lotion and other products for men. It was a smart financial move not to put all the company's eggs in one basket.

egg someone on
jemanden anspornen oder anstacheln
I didn't want to do it but my wife egged me on to write that book.

ENCYCLOPEDIA

be a walking encyclopedia
ein wandelndes Konversationslexikon sein
You can ask Nathaniel any question at all and he always knows the answer. He is a walking encyclopedia. He never runs out of things to say at a party.

END

her hair stood on end
ihr standen die Haare zu Berge
Her hair stood on end when she was driving down the mountain road and suddenly noticed that the car's brakes didn't work.

the end justifies the means
der Zweck heiligt die Mittel
I know that most politicians and revolutionaries say that the end justifies the means, but I have never believed in this philosophy.

her hair stood on end

be at the end of one's rope
nicht mehr aus noch ein wissen
I have done everything and I have tried everything and have said everything hoping that she would love me. But I see now that I have come to the end of my rope. She loves someone else.

go off the deep end
die Fassung verlieren, aus dem Häuschen geraten
You have to be careful what you say to the boss early on a Monday morning. He can go off the deep end at the drop of a hat.

make both ends meet
mit seinen Einkünften auskommen
She has four children and a husband that is out of work. Betty has a hard time each month making both ends meet. But she manages.

all's well that ends well
Ende gut, alles gut
Who cares about all the mistakes and failures in your past? Everything is okay now. That's what really matters. As Shakespeare wrote a long time ago: all's well that ends well.

ENEMY

be one's own worst enemy
sich selbst im Wege stehen, sich selbst am meisten schaden
He's not getting any higher on the ladder of success, because he's his own worst enemy.

be one's own worst enemy

ENGLISH

in plain English
auf gut deutsch, offen gesagt
You want to know what I think of his new book? Well, let me tell you in plain English. I think it stinks!

ENOUGH

oddly enough
seltsamerweise
He lost his job. He lost his wife. He lost his home and his car. But oddly enough he didn't lose his good sense of humour.

leave well enough alone
fünf gerade sein lassen, an etwas nicht rühren
The picture on the TV set is just fine. Don't touch anything. The colours are fine. Be good, Arthur, and leave well enough alone.

EQUAL

be without equal
seinesgleichen suchen
There are many perfumes on the market but this brand is truly without equal.

other things being equal
bei sonst gleichen Umständen
Other things being equal you should have a good chance of winning the race tomorrow. We wish you the best of luck, George.

be equal to the task
einer Aufgabe gewachsen sein
I am very glad that they picked Peter for this very important and dangerous job. He is the only man equal to the task.

be on equal footing with
auf gleicher Stufe stehen mit
The women managers in this company are on equal footing with the
men managers. The president wants it that way.

EVERYTHING

have everything
alles haben, was man sich nur wünschen kann
He is a very difficult man to buy a present for because he has everything.

mean everything to someone
jemandes ein und alles sein
"I love you, Helen," said Gene. "And you know that you mean absolutely everything to me."

EVIL

the root of all evil
die Wurzel allen Übels
They say that money is the root of all evil. Well, that's why I try to get
rid of my money as fast as I can.

choose the lesser of two evils
von zwei Übeln das kleinere wählen
Both political candidates weren't any good but we voted for the man
from the progressive party. We chose the lesser of two evils.

regard something as a necessary evil
etwas als notwendiges Übel betrachten
My brother regards paying income tax as a necessary evil.

EXCEPTION

the exception proves the rule
die Ausnahme bestätigt die Regel
Henry is almost always a bit drunk by eleven. He always drinks at the office. But today he was completely sober at eleven. It just goes to show that the exception proves the rule.

make an exception of someone
bei jemandem eine Ausnahme machen
I am very sorry, but if we made an exception of you in this matter, then we would have to make an exception of everyone. So you see, the answer is no. Please come back tomorrow during regular office hours. We can help you then.

take exception to a thing
an etwas Anstoß nehmen
I take exception to the fact that you think I didn't do a good job on this important project. I did. Everyone knows I did.

EYE

as far as the eye can see
soweit das Auge reicht
How much of this land belongs to you, Michael? As far as the eye can see and then some more beyond the horizon.

my eyes were bigger than my stomach
meine Augen waren größer als der Magen
Sitting at the dinner table, I helped myself to two pork chops, a small mountain of mashed potatoes with gravy; green peas, salad, and a big glass of wine. I finished the wine all right. But I couldn't finish the mashed potatoes. Once again, my eyes were bigger than my stomach. Next time I'll know better.

in the eyes of the law
vom Standpunkt des Gesetzes aus, laut Gesetz
Spitting on the sidewalk is still an offence in the eyes of the law.

in the twinkling of an eye
im Nu, im Handumdrehen
Barbara can empty a bottle of beer in the twinkling of an eye.

be a sight for sore eyes
eine Augenweide sein
I had been lost in the desert for two days without water. When I saw the oasis up ahead it was a sight for sore eyes.

catch someone's eye
jemandem ins Auge fallen
The woman in the bright red dress immediately caught George's eye.

cry one's eyes out
sich die Augen ausweinen
Every night for two weeks Ernest cried his eyes out over Uli.

have eyes in the back of one's head
Augen vorn und hinten haben
Our English teacher always knew what our class was doing. Sometimes we truly believed that she must have had eyes in the back of her head.

have eyes like a hawk
Augen wie ein Luchs haben
A thief never had a chance in that department store, because the house detective there had eyes like a hawk.

keep an eye on someone
ein wachsames Auge auf jemanden haben
My little boy was playing in the garden. I had to go to the supermarket to get something and so I asked my neighbour to keep an eye on him. He was playing so nicely.

keep an eye on things
ein wachsames Auge auf etwas haben
Our assistant manager is going to keep an eye on things here at the office when our big boss goes on holiday next week.

make eyes at someone
jemandem verliebte Blicke zuwerfen
I don't know who she is but that nice girl in the corner is making eyes at me. And you know what? I love it.

open one's eyes
die Augen aufmachen
Malcolm, open your eyes to the fact that you're not getting any younger. You can't go on doing such things any more.

ruin one's eyes
sich die Augen verderben
My mother always told me that I would ruin my eyes if I constantly read by candlelight (something I loved to do). And she was right.

see eye to eye with someone about something
mit jemandem derselben Meinung sein
My wife and I do not see eye to eye with each other about a lot of things, but we do agree on how to raise our children.

shut one's eyes to the facts
die Augen vor den Tatsachen verschließen
The bad thing about Robert is that he is able to shut his eyes to the facts concerning his alcoholism. He still has a long way to go before he realizes how serious his problem really is.

with the naked eye
mit bloßem Auge
You don't need a microscope to see it. You can see it clearly with the naked eye if you know where to look for it.

eye opener
ernüchterndes Erlebnis
It was an eye opener for me when I found out that my boss had hired another man to do the same work I was doing. And the thing was that this new man could do the work better than I could.

F

FACE

on the face of it
auf den ersten Blick, oberflächlich betrachtet
On the face of it this problem seems easy, but in fact it is more difficult than you can imagine.

a slap in the face
ein Schlag ins Gesicht
When my boss said to me that he didn't think I was suited for the job it was like a slap in the face to me.

keep a straight face
sich das Lachen verbeißen
I couldn't keep a straight face when the politician started talking about his plans for our city.

make faces
Gesichter schneiden, Grimassen schneiden
Mike made faces at the children's birthday party yesterday and made them laugh for a long, long time.

face the facts
sich mit den Tatsachen abfinden
Let's be honest and face the facts. Both of us have lost our jobs and there's little chance of finding new ones.

face the music
die Konsequenzen ziehen, die Folgen tragen
I told my father I would be home by ten. Now it's one o'clock in the morning. When I get home I'm going to have to face the music.

face up to one's problems
sich mit seinen Problemen auseinandersetzen
Gerry never runs away from his problems. He faces up to them.

take something at face value
etwas für bare Münze nehmen
Never take anything a politician says at face value.

FAIR

fair and square
offen und ehrlich
Gerald is fair and square in all his business dealings.

a fair-weather friend
ein Schön-Wetter-Freund
If you didn't have any money, Henry, he would leave you tomorrow.
He's just a fair-weather friend.

FALL

fall flat
scheitern, keine Wirkung haben
My party fell flat last night because only a couple of people showed up.
And then my jokes fell flat because no one liked them.

fall for someone
sich Hals über Kopf verlieben
Ernest fell for Ulrike in a big way the first time he saw her.

fall for something
auf etwas hereinfallen
Peter fell for one of the oldest tricks in the world: a get-rich-quick
scheme.

fall in love with someone
sich in jemanden verlieben
Almost everyone knows the story of how Romeo fell in love with Ju-
liet.

fall in love with someone

fall into disuse
außer Gebrauch kommen
Slowly but surely the mechanical typewriter is falling into disuse. The same thing applies to electric typewriters.

fall into line
sich einreihen, sich fügen, sich anpassen
There is only one way to work in this company: the boss's way. If you don't fall into line you can start looking for a new job.

fall to pieces
in Stücke fallen, die Fassung verlieren
Olga lost her nerve at the last moment and fell to pieces.

have something to fall back on
an etwas einen Rückhalt haben
Yes, it's always nice to know that you have something to fall back on when the times are rough: like a million dollars for example.

FAMILY

run in the family
in der Familie liegen
My brothers and sisters are geniuses. It just runs in the family.

start a family
eine Familie gründen
My girlfriend and I want to get married and start a family.

be a family man
ein guter Hausvater sein
He used to be a famous playboy but now he's a family man.

be in the family way
schwanger sein, guter Hoffnung sein
My sister is in the family way again. Her husband is very happy.

FAR

far and wide
weit und breit
I looked far and wide for a small apartment in the city but I wasn't able to find one. I live out in the country now.

so far, so good
so weit, so gut
An optimist fell off a tall building. As he was falling down he winked to everyone and said, "So far, so good."

be a far cry from
weit entfernt sein von, etwas ganz anderes sein als
His present book is a far cry from the one he wrote last year.

go too far
es zu bunt treiben
You went too far in all the things you did, Ernest. That's one of the reasons why your wife left you.

FAT

live off the fat of the land
ein üppiges Leben führen, auf großem Fuße leben
Algernon is a multi-millionaire and he enjoys living off the fat of the land.

FATHER

like father, like son
wie der Vater, so der Sohn
My father likes to drink a lot. I like to drink a lot. My father is fat and so am I. We both like to read books. My mother always says, "Like father, like son."

FEATHER

birds of a feather flock together
gleich und gleich gesellt sich gern
They say that misery loves company. And it's true. I feel miserable, my neighbour feels miserable, and a lot of my friends feel miserable. We get together in the evenings and talk about our problems. "Birds of a feather flock together," I always say to them when they come over.

that's a feather in your cap
darauf kannst du stolz sein
Helen is the first woman to become a president in our company. That's really a feather in her cap.

be as light as a feather
federleicht sein
Although she weighs over 200 pounds, she is as light as a feather on the dance floor.

feather one's own nest
sein Schäfchen ins trockene bringen
The company president doesn't care if the company goes bankrupt.
All he's interested in is feathering his own nest.

FEED

be fed up with something
etwas satt haben, von etwas die Nase voll haben
I was so fed up with the long hours, the small salary, the lack of appreciation at work that I quit my job yesterday.

FEEL

feel bad about something
etwas bedauern
I feel bad about you losing your job with the company.

feel for someone
mit jemandem Mitleid haben
He lost his job and his wife and his car and his home last week. I really feel for him.

feel lost
sich verloren vorkommen
Patrick feels lost now that his girlfriend has left him.

feel on top of the world
auf der Höhe sein, sich obenauf fühlen
A couple of days ago Patrick met a new girl at a party. They are both in love. Patrick is feeling on top of the world.

feel sorry for oneself
sich bemitleiden
I know that feeling sorry for yourself is one of the easiest things to do in the world when things are going badly, Ralph, but it is also one of the worst things that you can do to yourself.

FEET

be on one's feet again
wieder auf den Beinen sein
Don't worry about Frank. He'll be back on his feet again very soon.
He is a man of many talents.

be swept off one's feet
sich hinreißen lassen
Helen was swept off her feet by his charm and his arguments.

have two left feet
zwei linke Hände haben
Mike is a nice guy and we all like him. But sometimes when we ask him
to do something he's just impossible, because he has two left feet.

FEW

few and far between
dünn gesät, vereinzelt
Jobs are few and far between in this part of the country.

FICTION

truth is stranger than fiction
die Wirklichkeit kann seltsamer sein als ein Roman
When I read some of the stories that they print in the newspapers, I
really believe sometimes that truth is really stranger than fiction.

FILL

have one's fill of something
die Nase voll von etwas haben
I am a businessman and I have to travel a lot. I eat out in restaurants.
But let me tell you, I've had my fill of eating in restaurants. I would
like to have some nice home-cooked meals.

fill a need
eine Lücke ausfüllen
They say that a sure way to success is to find a need and fill it.

fill the bill
allen Ansprüchen genügen
I really need a screwdriver to repair this thing but that small coin you gave me fills the bill, too.

FINGER

have a finger in the pie
die Hand im Spiel haben
I can't prove it but I'm fairly sure that Alphonse has a finger in the pie. I know that he has something to do with what is happening at the office.

have a finger in the pie

keep one's fingers crossed
den Daumen drücken
"I'm going to my job interview now, Lance," said Gina to her husband. "I hope I get the job. Keep your fingers crossed for me." "I will!"

not lift a finger
keinen Finger rühren, keinen Schlag tun
Helga has a most unusual husband. He does all the housework. Her husband doesn't even want her to lift a finger.

slip through someone's fingers
jemandem durch die Lappen gehen
I feel so miserable today, because I let the chance of a lifetime slip through my fingers this afternoon.

have something at one's fingertips
etwas intuitiv können, wissen
She is the best secretary in the company. She never has to go and look up a customer's records. She has all the information right at her fingertips.

FIRE

out of the frying pan and into the fire
vom Regen in die Traufe
They asked me why I did something crazy like that. I answered them by saying that jumping out of the frying pan and into the fire gave me a feeling of freedom.

add fuel to the fire
Öl ins Feuer gießen
He's mad and angry and unhappy as it is today. Don't go adding fuel to the fire by telling him that you wrecked the car.

fan the fires
das Feuer schüren
The people out there are angry enough. Don't fan the fires by speaking too openly. We don't want any trouble.

fight fire with fire
mit gleicher Waffe zurückschlagen
There is only one way to beat them at their own game. And that is by doing exactly the same thing that they did to us. You have to fight fire with fire if you want to win.

set something on fire
etwas in Brand stecken
Gerald said that he didn't want to set the world on fire. All he wanted to do was to put a flame in Helga's heart.

FIX

be in a fix
in der Klemme sitzen
I was lucky because I had a good friend who helped me when I was in a fix last month.

fix someone for that
jemandem etwas vergelten, heimzahlen
Mike said that he was going to fix his boss for firing him.

fix a price
einen Preis festsetzen
We fixed a price for our new computer that made everyone happy.

fix dinner
das Abendessen zubereiten
She fixes dinner for her family every evening at six.

fix the car
das Auto reparieren
The mechanic around the corner fixed my car last week, and didn't charge me too much for it, either.

fix the jury
die Geschworenen bestechen
The only reason that he is a free man today is because his father has a lot of money and was able to fix the jury.

FLY

a fly in the ointment
ein Haar in der Suppe
It was a wonderful party last night. But David got very drunk. That was the only fly in the ointment.

harm not a fly
keiner Fliege etwas zuleide tun
I don't even know how you could think such a thing about him. He is such a good man. He wouldn't harm a fly.

as the crow flies
in der Luftlinie
How far is it from La Mesa to El Cajon? Well, as the crow flies it's about a couple of miles.

come through with flying colours
sich glänzend bewähren, mit großem Erfolg absolvieren
We honestly didn't think our son would pass his university exams. But he came through with flying colours.

fly into a rage
in die Luft gehen, in Wut geraten
Alan flies into a rage every time his car doesn't start in the mornings.

FOOD

food for thought
Stoff zum Nachdenken
Sinting Lai has written a very interesting book on philosophy. There is plenty of food for thought in his book.

FOOL

there is no fool like an old fool
Alter schützt vor Torheit nicht
You would think that Matthew would know better than to do such a crazy thing at his age. But it just goes to show that there is no fool like an old fool.

food for thought

be nobody's fool
nicht auf den Kopf gefallen sein, nicht von gestern sein
Ulrike Manlik is a smart woman and she knows how to take care of herself. Everyone knows that she's nobody's fool.

make a fool of oneself
sich lächerlich machen
Martha made a fool of herself by saying that Christopher Columbus discovered America in 1832. Everyone knew that it was in 1492. But she kept on saying that she was right.

make a fool of someone
jemanden zum Narren halten
You made a fool of me in front of all those people, Judith. I will never be able to forgive you for that.

play the fool
den Narren spielen, sich närrisch verhalten
Be serious for once in your life, Jennifer, and stop playing the fool. We all know there's more to you than meets the eye.

fool someone
jemanden hinters Licht führen, jemanden übers Ohr hauen
They say that you can fool some of the people all of the time; all of the people some of the time; but you can't fool all of the people all of the time.

FOOT

get off on the right foot
einen guten Anfang machen
Today is going to be a good day, because I got off on the right foot this morning.

put one's best foot forward
sich von der besten Seite zeigen
If you want to get that job with that company, Richard, you are going to have to put your best foot forward at the interview.

put one's foot down
energisch eingreifen, ein Machtwort sprechen
When the pupils in the class started making too much noise, the teacher put her foot down. The class was quiet in no time.

put one's foot in one's mouth
ins Fettnäpfchen treten
Ernest is always putting his foot in his mouth by telling jokes at parties that hurt other people's feelings.

wait on someone hand and foot
jemanden von hinten und vorne bedienen
Horst leads the life of a king. His wife waits on him hand and foot. He never has to do anything.

foot the bill
die Zeche bezahlen
I'm the manager of this office and when my employees make mistakes I have to foot the bill when the president wants to know why things went wrong.

FREE

free and easy
ungezwungen, ungeniert
I like his way of dancing. It's so free and easy.

be free of charge
kostenlos sein
The tickets for the open-air concert tonight are free of charge.

get off scot-free
ohne Bestrafung davonkommen
The bank robber got off scot-free, because he had a good lawyer.

set someone free
jemanden befreien, auf freien Fuß setzen
The kidnappers set the man free after they got the ransom money.

FRIEND

a friend in need is a friend indeed
in der Not erkennt man seine wahren Freunde
Helen helped me when I had no money, no food to eat, no place to
live. It's true that a friend in need is a friend indeed.

FUN

for the fun of it
zum Spaß, spaßeshalber
I'm learning the piano at age forty just for the fun of it.

have fun
Spaß haben, sich gut amüsieren
We had a lot of fun at the party last night.

say something in fun
etwas im Scherz sagen
I didn't mean it seriously, Pamela. I just said that in fun.

G_____

GAB

have the gift of the gab
ein gutes Mundwerk haben
Patrick can talk for hours on end. He never bores or tires anyone with
what he says. He really has the gift of the gab.

GAIN

nothing ventured, nothing gained
nichts gewagt, nichts gewonnen
They say it is better to have tried and failed than not to have tried at all. I always say, "Nothing ventured, nothing gained."

GALLERY

play to the gallery
nach Effekt haschen
He is an actor through and through. He is always playing to the gallery wherever he is.

GAME

the game is up
das Spiel ist aus
"Okay, let's go Mr. van Voorst," said the policeman to the banker. "The game is up. We know you've been taking the money."

beat someone at his own game
jemanden mit seinen eigenen Waffen schlagen
If you want to make a lot of money in this line of work, you have to beat the competition at their own game.

GET

don't get me wrong
verstehen Sie mich nicht falsch
"Listen, Mike," I said to my good friend, "and don't get me wrong. All I'm saying is that I can't loan you the money today."

I don't get it
das verstehe ich nicht, das kapiere ich nicht
I'm sorry, but I don't get what you're trying to tell me.

get along with someone
sich mit jemandem gut verstehen, mit jemandem gut auskommen
The nice thing about Bill is that he gets along with everyone.

get around to doing something
dazu kommen, etwas zu tun
Yesterday I finally got around to doing my housework.

get away with something
ungeschoren davonkommen
He was lucky. He got away with not doing his homework yesterday, because the teacher didn't collect the notebooks.

get back at someone
sich an jemandem rächen
If it's the last thing I do this year, I'm going to get back at him for what he did to me.

get by
durchkommen, sich durchschlagen
Don't worry about me. I'll get by somehow in this world.

get by without something
ohne etwas fertig werden, ohne etwas auskommen
Mr. Brown has a drinking problem. He can't get by without a glass of wine in the mornings.

get down to brass tacks
zur Sache kommen
"Okay, we've talked enough about the weather and the political situation. Let's get down to brass tacks now. How much do you want for this car?"

get going
an die Arbeit gehen, sich auf den Weg machen
"I have to get going now because I want to get going on my new book," said the famous writer to his friends.

get going

get nowhere with someone
bei jemandem nichts erreichen
Ernest told Uli how sorry he was about everything and how he would change and how he had already changed and how he missed her and how he loved her.
But it got him nowhere with her.

get off lightly
mit einem blauen Auge davonkommen
The policeman warned me not to drive so fast the next time. He didn't give me a speeding ticket. I got off lightly this time.

get on in years
in die Jahre kommen
I'll have to buy a new car soon. My old one is getting on in years.

get to the point
zur Sache kommen, sich kurz fassen
What are you trying to say? Get to the point! I haven't got all day,
Judy.

get word
Nachricht bekommen
I got word yesterday that an old friend of mine is in town.

GHOST

not a ghost of a chance
nicht die geringste Aussicht
Fred didn't have a ghost of a chance of getting that new job, but he
applied for it anyway.

GIVE

give a talk
eine Rede halten
Paula Kellner gave a talk about bears in Alaska.

give chase to someone
Jagd auf jemanden machen
The police gave chase to the three boys who had thrown snowballs at
their car.

give in
nachgeben
I didn't want another piece of cake for dessert, but my hostess insisted
and then I finally gave in.

give oneself away
sich verraten
The secret agent was trained very carefully so that he wouldn't give
himself away when he was in a foreign country.

90

give oneself up
sich freiwillig stellen, sich ergeben
Sam Brown, the famous bank robber, didn't want to run and hide from the police any more. He finally gave himself up.

give someone a piece of one's mind
jemandem gehörig die Meinung sagen
I think it's just horrible the way our neighbour treats her children. The next time I see her I'm going to give her a piece of my mind.

GLOVE

fit like a glove
wie angegossen passen
This new coat that I bought for myself fits me like a glove.

handle someone with kid gloves
jemanden mit Glacéhandschuhen anfassen
Jennifer lost her boyfriend to another woman. She has been crying all week. Her friends are handling her with kid gloves.

GO

from the word go
von Anfang an
Linda was a genius at school from the word go.

be always on the go
immer auf Trab sein
Michael is rarely at home. He's always somewhere else. At meetings, at parties, at the cinema. He is a restless man and that is probably why he is always on the go.

have a go at a thing
sein Glück mit etwas versuchen
I've never played roulette in my life, but tonight at the casino I'm going to have a go at it.

go without saying
das versteht sich von selbst
It goes without saying that cigarette smoking is bad for your health.

be going on thirty
auf die dreißig zugehen
How old is he? 28 or 29! In any case, he's going on thirty.

go broke
pleite machen
I'm going to go broke if I keep on spending so much money.

go by the book
nach den Vorschriften handeln
Bill Pierce is a policeman that always goes by the book.

go in for something
sich für etwas interessieren, etwas gern tun
Dorothy goes in for astronomy and Chinese cooking and the latest French fashions.

go on the air
die Sendung beginnen
Everyone in the studio audience has to be quiet when we go on the air at seven this evening.

go out of one's way
sich besondere Mühe geben
My teacher really went out of his way to help me with the problems I was having with English verbs.

go over well
gut aufgenommen werden, Anklang finden
Gisela Bolte's speech at the women's club last night went over well. They even gave her a standing ovation.

go steady
eine feste Freundin oder einen festen Freund haben
Carol and Sidney like each other very much. They don't go out with anybody else, because they are going steady.

go through a great deal
viel durchmachen
His nerves are bad because he has been through a great deal this past year.

go through with a thing
etwas zu Ende führen
The bosses like Nancy Newman, because once she starts a new project she always goes through with it.

go to pieces
die Fassung verlieren
Her husband went to pieces when he found out that his wife was in a bad car accident. But everything turned out okay.

go well with something
zu etwas passen, mit etwas gut harmonieren
The nice thing about the colour of money is that it goes well with everything.

have nothing to go on
keinen Anhalt haben
The police don't even know where to start in this matter, because they have absolutely nothing to go on.

let it go at that
es dabei bewenden lassen
I was late five times last month. My boss called me into the office and warned me. I was lucky. He let it go at that.

be touch and go
auf des Messers Schneide stehen
It was touch and go for about ten minutes whether our pilot would be able to land the plane safely during the snowstorm.

GOOD

be up to no good
Böses im Schilde führen
As usual, our neighbour's boys have been up to no good.

good for you
gut gemacht, bravo!
"I got the job, Helen!" "Good for you, Ernest!"

have a good time
sich gut amüsieren
We always have a good time when we go to the Flamingo Club.

make good
Erfolg haben, es zu etwas bringen
My parents worked long and hard and that's why they made good in this country.

too much of a good thing
zuviel des Guten
I have always liked the comedian who said that too much of a good thing is ... wonderful!

GOOSE

cook someone's goose
jemanden erledigen, jemandem die Suppe versalzen
Look what he did to me! He's ruined me. I'm going to cook his goose for this. He'll be sorry that he ever met me.

get goose pimples
eine Gänsehaut kriegen
I even get goose pimples on my nose when I hear her sing.

GRAIN

take something with a grain of salt
etwas nicht zu ernst nehmen, nicht so genau nehmen
You have to remember that Patrick is a fisherman. And that is why it is a good idea to take his stories with a grain of salt.

GRAPEVINE

hear something through the grapevine
ein Gerücht hören
I'm not really sure about what's happening, but I heard it through the grapevine that they want to close down this company.

GRIND

be a grind
eine Plackerei sein
I absolutely hate going to work in the mornings. It's no fun. It's no picnic, that's for sure. It's a grind. That's all it is.

grind one's teeth
mit den Zähnen knirschen
Janet had to grind her teeth when she heard all those lies that they were telling about her at the office.

keep one's nose to the grindstone
schuften, pausenlos arbeiten, sich abmühen
My father always used to tell me that I could achieve my ambitions and goals in life by keeping my nose to the grindstone.

GROUND

cover a lot of ground
viel behandeln
Our professor covered a lot of ground this semester. We now know a lot about the history of the United States.

gain ground
an Boden gewinnen
Ernest is sad because his love isn't gaining any ground with Uli.

get off the ground
in Schwung kommen, in Gang kommen
Last night's party never got off the ground. It was a flop.

stand one's ground
sich behaupten, seinen Mann stehen, nicht nachgeben
My mother always used to tell me that if I was right and I believed that I was right that I should stand my ground.

stand one's ground

GUESS

take a guess
raten
The geography teacher asked me how many people lived in New York. I didn't really know. I took a guess. I said around ten million. The teacher said that that was correct.

I guess so
ich nehme es wohl an
"Do you think it would be all right for me to have another glass of this red wine before the guests come, Dear?" "I guess so."

GUN

jump the gun
vorzeitig anfangen
Don't jump the gun yet, Steve. You still don't have the contract in your hand. Start work only when the ink is dry on the paper.

stick to one's guns
von seinen Grundsätzen nicht abweichen
People who stick to their guns in life do not have it easy.

GUTTER

wind up in the gutter
in der Gosse enden
You'll wind up in the gutter some day, Ray, if you keep on smoking and drinking and running around with the wrong people.

H

HAND

hands off!
Hände weg!
"Hands off the merchandise!" said the shop assistant to the teenagers that were playing with the crystal glasses.

hands up!
Hände hoch!
"Hands up!" said the bank robber to the teller. "This is a stick-up."

be an old hand at
ein alter Praktiker sein in
Jane is an old hand at sewing on buttons for children's coats.

be close at hand
vor der Tür stehen
Father's birthday is close at hand. I have to get him a present.

give someone a hand
jemandem Beifall klatschen; jemandem helfen
The audience gave the singer a big hand, because he sang so beautifully.
My neighbour asked me to give him a hand with the heavy packages. And I did. After all, what are neighbours for?

have time on one's hands
Zeit zum Vertrödeln haben, viel Zeit haben
I lost my job last week. So now I've got a lot of time on my hands. I don't like it. I wish I had a job.

take the law into one's own hands
sich selbst Recht verschaffen
In the old days in the American West people often took the law into their own hands.

try one's hand
sich in etwas versuchen, sein Glück mit etwas versuchen
I tried my hand at baking a cake but it didn't turn out so well.

wait on someone hand and foot
jemanden von hinten und vorne bedienen
He leads the life of a prince. His wife waits on him hand and foot.

win hands down
spielend leicht gewinnen
Our team is going to win that match hands down.

I have to hand it to her
das muß ich ihr lassen
"I have to hand it to her," said the boss. "Betty is the fastest and the best worker in our company."

wait on someone hand and foot

catch someone red-handed
jemanden auf frischer Tat ertappen
The police caught the safecracker red-handed.

be handy at something
geschickt sein in etwas
My brother is really handy at repairing things around the house.

come in handy
nützlich sein
This pocketknife will come in handy when I go camping.

HAT

at the drop of a hat
bei dem geringsten Anlaß
Gerald is ready to fight at the drop of a hat if someone says the wrong
thing to him or about his wife.

keep something under one's hat
etwas geheimhalten, etwas für sich behalten
Don't tell anyone about what happened here this morning. I want you
to keep this information under your hat.

pass the hat around
Geld einsammeln
It's Bruce's birthday next week. His friends at work are going to pass
the hat around and buy him a nice present.

talk through one's hat
Unsinn reden
Barbara said that the Earth is the fourth planet from the sun.
Everyone knows that she's just talking through her hat.

HEAD

unable to make heads or tails of something
aus etwas nicht klug werden
I couldn't make heads or tails of the report that he wrote.

go to one's head
jemandem zu Kopf steigen
All that fast money went to Gerald's head.

head over heels
Hals über Kopf
Barbara was head over heals in love with Andreas.

head for the hills
sich aus dem Staube machen
I headed for the hills yesterday when my husband came home angry
from work.

HEART

after one's own heart
nach jemandes Herzen
Gene doesn't smoke, doesn't drink, docsn't yell at his wife or children. He is kind and gentle and likes to read good books. He is a man
after my own heart.

from the bottom of one's heart
aus tiefstem Herzen
I want to thank everyone from the bottom of my heart for such a lovely
birthday present. Thank you.

break someone's heart
jemandem das Herz brechen
She broke his heart when she told him she didn't love him.

have a heart of stone
ein steinernes Herz haben
They say that to have a heart of stone is bad enough. But what is worse than that is to have no heart at all.

know by heart
auswendig kennen
I know the names of all the American presidents by heart.

lose heart
den Mut verlieren
He had a lot of troubles and problems but he never lost heart.

pour one's heart out to someone
jemandem das Herz ausschütten
I have a good friend. He always listens to me when I'm in trouble. I can easily pour my heart out to him. I feel better then.

speak from the heart
frisch von der Leber weg sprechen
It's always an emotional experience to hear him talk, because he always speaks from the heart. He is a rare man indeed.

HEEL

cool one's heels
jemanden zappeln lassen
The boss let me cool my heels for a couple of days before he would talk to me about increasing my salary.

take to one's heels
die Beine in die Hand nehmen, fliehen
Edward took to his heels before the trouble really started.

HEM

hem and haw
sich krümmen und winden, herumdrucksen
The husband hemmed and hawed when his wife asked him why he had come home so late the night before.

HERE

be neither here nor there
nicht zur Sache gehören
"That's very interesting, Janet," said her husband, "But it isn't relevant to what we're talking about. It's neither here nor there. The important thing is how do we get the money."

HIDE-AND-SEEK

play hide-and-seek
Versteck spielen
When we were children we loved playing hide-and-seek in the woods.

HILL

as old as the hills
uralt
We like Ernie's jokes a lot but they are as old as the hills.

be over the hill
die besten Jahre hinter sich haben
Frank used to be a great singer. He still sings well but is over the hill. He should stop. At least that's what I think.

HINT

drop a broad hint
einen Wink mit dem Zaunpfahl geben
She dropped a broad hint by saying she liked French perfume.

take a hint
einen Wink verstehen
"Here's your hat! What's your hurry?" said the host to his guest. But the guest couldn't take a hint. He stayed a while longer.

hint at something
auf etwas anspielen
What are you hinting at? Tell me! I want to know. Speak clearly. Don't play games with me.

HIT

be hard hit by something
schwer getroffen sein durch etwas
I was hard hit by my wife's going off with another man.

hit below the belt
unter der Gürtellinie treffen, unfair handeln
"He's old and fat and bald. Don't vote for him," said the politician. But the voters knew that the politician was hitting below the belt. They didn't listen to him.

hit it off with someone
sich mit jemandem gut verstehen
Michael and Christine hit it off with each other immediately.

hit the mark
ins Schwarze treffen
That last comment of his about the boss hit the mark.

HITCH

there's a hitch to it
die Sache hat einen Haken
That business deal of yours sounds good and it looks good, too. I'm just wondering if there's a hitch to it somewhere.

go off without a hitch
sich reibungslos abwickeln
I'm glad to hear that your business deal went off without a hitch.

hitchhike
trampen
The cheapest way to travel in the United States is to hitchhike.

HOLE

be in a hole
in Schulden stecken, in der Klemme sitzen
I spent too much money last year on wine, women and song. And now I'm in a hole and I don't know how to get out of it.

punch holes in something
etwas bekritteln, an einer Sache herumnörgeln
We have a good company here. The organization is effective, but for some reason a lot of the employees are always punching holes in the way the company is run.

HOOK

by hook or by crook
so oder so
"We're going to get that contract by hook or by crook," said the dishonest businessman.

fall for something hook, line, and sinker
auf etwas ganz schön hereinfallen
The rich oilman from Texas was extremely naive. When he went to Paris, a Frenchman told him that the Eiffel Tower was for sale. The Texan fell for the story hook, line, and sinker.

HOPE

get one's hopes up too high
seine Erwartungen zu hoch spannen
"You have a chance, maybe even a good chance, of getting that job," said the father to his son, "but don't get your hopes up too high."

where there's life, there's hope
nur Mut!
Horst was an optimist and he would never let things in life get him down. "Where there's life, there's hope," he would always say when the situation was difficult.

hope against hope
weiterhoffen, wo nichts mehr zu retten ist
Ernest was hoping against hope that Ulrike would come back to him again.

HORSE

be a horse of a different colour
eine ganz andere Sache sein
Working hard at the job you have is a good way of earning a living. But gambling in Las Vegas, well, that's a horse of a different colour.

beat a dead horse
Interesse für eine erledigte Sache zu wecken versuchen
Nobody is interested in her plans for the future, but she still keeps talking about them. She's beating a dead horse.

straight from the horse's mouth
etwas aus erster Hand haben
"How do you know that the boss is quitting his job, Henry?" "I got the information straight from the horse's mouth. The boss told me himself yesterday."

beat a dead horse

put the cart before the horse
das Pferd beim Schwanze aufzäumen
He wanted me to give him the money for the television set first. Then
he would bring it. I told him that was putting the cart before the horse.
First the television set and then the money.

HOUSETOP

shout something from the housetops
etwas an die große Glocke hängen
When Theresa inherited a million dollars from her grandfather, she
kept quiet about it. She was smart and didn't go shouting it from the
housetops.

I

ICE

break the ice
das Eis brechen
Kenneth has no trouble at all in starting a conversation. He simply
breaks the ice by smiling while he introduces himself. Then he tells a
short joke and everybody is laughing.

cut no ice with somebody
niemandem imponieren
I don't care if you have a big house, a fantastic job, and a lot of money.
That doesn't cut any ice with me.

skate on thin ice
ein heikles Thema berühren
You're going to be skating on thin ice tomorrow when you ask the boss
for more money for the work that you do, Frederick.

IDEA

put ideas in someone's head
jemandem einen Floh ins Ohr setzen
"Why do you think you should quit your job and sell the house?" the wife asked her husband. "Who's been putting those ideas in your head?"

what's the big idea?
was soll denn das?
What's the big idea of telling everyone you know that I lost my job yesterday?

IMAGE

be the very image of someone
jemandem wie aus dem Gesicht geschnitten sein
Our third son is the very image of his father.

IMAGINE

imagine that!
stellen Sie sich das mal vor!
George is now the president of his own computer company. Imagine that! And he used to be the slowest student in mathematics.

IN

in a word
mit einem Wort
"Do I get the job or not?" "In a word: No!"

know the ins and outs
alle Schliche kennen
James knows the ins and outs of selling frying pans door to door.

have it in someone
das Zeug dazu haben
We all know that Betty has it in her to become a good singer.

be in for it
sein Teil abbekommen
When the teacher finds out that Mary did it, she is going to be in for it.

be all in
völlig erschöpft sein
After working in the office for ten hours Jim is usually all in by the time he gets home.

turn in
schlafen gehen
I didn't watch TV last night. I turned in early. I was tired.

INCH

give him an inch and he'll take a mile
gibt man ihm den kleinen Finger, so nimmt er gleich die ganze Hand
That's the trouble with your so-called friends. You help them a little and they want more and more. Typical. Give them an inch and they'll take a mile.

inch by inch
Schritt für Schritt
I'm sure you know the way to solve all your problems, Gerald. Remember that yard by yard it's hard, but inch by inch it's a cinch (it's easy).

INFANCY

be in its infancy
in den Kinderschuhen stecken
Research in this field of medicine is still in its infancy.

INSIDE

know something inside out
etwas in- und auswendig kennen
I've lived here for twenty years. I know this town inside out.

turn inside out
das Innere nach außen kehren
I always turn my trousers inside out before I put them into the washing machine.

IOU

give someone an IOU
jemandem einen Schuldschein geben
He lost all his money playing poker with the boys last night. He even had to give one of them an IOU.

J

JACK OF ALL TRADES

jack of all trades
Hansdampf in allen Gassen
Alan will always get by in life, because he is a jack of all trades. He can find a job almost anywhere.

jaywalk

JAYWALK

jaywalk
an unerlaubter Stelle die Straße überqueren
Julia rarely waits for a green light. She likes to jaywalk. It saves her a
lot of time. One of these days, though, she is going to have that run-
down feeling.

JILT

jilt someone
jemanden sitzenlassen, jemandem einen Korb geben
She knew that he had jilted her when he didn't show up in time to pick
her up to go to the big party. She was sad.

JOKE

take a joke
Spaß vertragen
The nice thing about Ernest is that he knows how to take a joke. However, there was a time when he couldn't take a joke.

it's no joke
es ist nicht zum Lachen
You're laughing and you think it's funny. But let me tell you, Ann, it's no joke to know that my boyfriend has left me for good.

be the butt of a joke
die Zielscheibe eines Witzes sein
Ernest has a great sense of humour. He doesn't mind it when he's the butt of a joke. He usually laughs the hardest himself.

get the joke
den Witz verstehen
Can you explain it to me again, Frank. I didn't get the joke.

play a joke on someone
jemandem einen Streich spielen
We played a joke on him at breakfast time by putting salt into the sugar bowl. We know he always takes sugar with his tea.

be only joking
nur einen Witz machen wollen
Don't be angry, Bill. He was only joking. He didn't want to offend you in any way, shape or form. Now, let's forget it.

JUDGE

be no judge of something
sich auf etwas nicht verstehen
You'll have to ask an expert, Martha. I'm no judge of diamonds and emeralds. They might be real, though.

one can't judge a book by its cover
der Schein trügt
And everyone thought they were such a happy family. It just goes to show that one can't judge a book by its cover.

JUMP

jump at the chance
die Gelegenheit beim Schopf packen
His company offered him a job in Africa. He didn't think twice. He jumped at the chance right away.

jump down someone's throat
jemandem über den Mund fahren
You don't have to jump down my throat just because I forgot to buy the coffee at the supermarket this afternoon.

jump to conclusions
voreilige Schlüsse ziehen
Now listen to me Jeanette. Just because you didn't get a bonus this month doesn't mean anything. Don't go jumping to conclusions. Maybe the boss just forgot about it. That's all.

K _____

KEEP

for keeps
auf immer und ewig
When Michael left Germany we all knew it was for keeps.

keep it up!
nur weiter so!
You've been doing excellent work at school, Frank. Keep it up!

keep an eye on someone
ein wachsames Auge auf jemanden haben
I'm going to the supermarket in ten minutes. Could you keep an eye on the children while I'm gone. I won't be long.

keep body and soul together
Leib und Seele zusammenhalten
Dorothy is an artist and lives in Paris. She is so poor that she hardly has enough money to keep body and soul together.

keep from laughing
sich das Lachen verbeißen
I can't keep from laughing when I see the boss wearing his yellow trousers.

keep in mind
im Gedächtnis behalten
I want all of you to keep in mind that we will be guests in his home. So I want all of you to be on your best behaviour.

keep in touch with someone
mit jemandem in Verbindung bleiben
She lives in San Francisco now. No, not in California. On the island of Ibiza. But we still keep in touch with each other.

keep late hours
lange aufbleiben, spät zu Bett gehen
Yes, Ernest is a night owl. He always keeps late hours. He says that he can do his best work then.

keep one's eyes peeled
scharf aufpassen
"Keep your eyes peeled when you're driving through the mountains this time of year. It's very dangerous with all the snow," said the father to his son.

keep someone company
jemandem Gesellschaft leisten
My neighbours kept me company in the evenings while my husband and children were away.

keep to oneself
Gesellschaft meiden
Olga rarely goes out anywhere. For as long as I've known her, she has always kept to herself.

keep up appearances
den Schein wahren
He has lost his house and his job and his wife and all his money. But he still keeps up appearances by driving around in his big car and drinking champagne in expensive clubs.

keep up with the Joneses
mit jedem Schritt halten wollen
Every time our neighbours buy a new car, we buy a new car, too. I know it's crazy but my husband says it's important to keep up with the Joneses.

KICK

get a kick out of something
seinen Spaß haben an etwas
My husband gets a kick out of going bowling Friday nights.

KILL

if looks could kill
wenn Blicke töten könnten
"If looks could kill, Martha," said Jim, "then you would be a mass murderer tonight."

kill two birds with one stone
zwei Fliegen mit einer Klappe schlagen
I had to fly to Paris on business. I took my wife along, because she had
never seen Paris before. That way I was able to kill two birds with one
stone. I mixed business with pleasure.

KISS

kiss and make up
sich versöhnen
Once in a while my wife and I have arguments. But we always kiss and
make up afterwards.

kiss someone good-bye
jemandem einen Abschiedskuß geben
He was sad. He was crying. He kissed her good-bye for the last time.
And the both of them knew it was the last time.

KNOW

be in the know
im Bilde sein
I found out about the plan last night, Sharon. So, you don't have to tell
me all about it. I'm in the know.

not that I know of
nicht, daß ich wüßte
"Is Mr. Jones going to be in town this evening?" "Not that I know of,
sir."

know all the answers
ein Besserwisser sein
"Look, Kevin. Nobody is asking you your opinion. We all know that
you know all the answers. So just go away, please."

know one's way around
sich auskennen
I lived in New York for ten years and that's why I know my way
around in that city so well.

know something like the palm of one's hand
etwas wie seine Westentasche kennen
I know Manhattan like the palm of my hand. And so does she.

know the ropes
den Rummel kennen, sich auskennen
He's been a car salesman for twenty years and knows the ropes.

know what's what
nicht auf den Kopf gefallen sein
He's been at the job for only three weeks, but he already knows what's
what.

not know someone from Adam
nicht die geringste Ahnung haben, wer jemand ist
"Is that Mr. Carruthers over there, Patricia?" "He might be, but I
don't know him from Adam," I replied.

L

LABOUR

labour of love
eine Arbeit, die man gern beziehungsweise unentgeltlich tut
He wrote that book on the history of his family more as a labour of
love than anything else.

LADDER

work one's way up the ladder
von der Pike auf dienen
George is now general manager of this company. He got there because he started working his way up the ladder 15 years ago.

LADY

lady killer
Herzensbrecher
"Jane, do you think Michael has strong sex appeal toward women?"
"Yes, I do. He is a real lady killer."

lady's man
Frauenheld
Jason likes to be with women more than with men. He's been a lady's man ever since I've known him.

landlady
Hauswirtin, Vermieterin
My landlady raises the rent for this apartment every three years.

leading lady
Hauptdarstellerin
Andrea van Tassel is the leading lady in our next film.

LAMB

be gentle as a lamb
sanft wie ein Lamm sein
Our dog looks big and dangerous but he's really gentle as a lamb.

LAND

the land of unlimited opportunities
das Land der unbegrenzten Möglichkeiten
My parents came to the United States when they were young, because they believed it to be the land of unlimited opportunities.

check the lay of the land
sehen, wie der Hase läuft
I wanted to check the lay of the land before I went in to talk to the boss.

land a job
Arbeit bekommen
Olga finally landed a job in a department store as a sales clerk.

LAST

at long last
endlich, schließlich
I can't believe it myself, but I think it's true. This is at long last true love.

last but not least
nicht zuletzt
"And now, ladies and gentlemen," said the woman, "last but not least – Mr. George Abercrombie, our guest speaker for today."

last for ages
eine Ewigkeit dauern
The trouble is that one of his speeches can last for ages.

as a last resort
als letzter Ausweg, wenn alle Stränge reißen
The police only use tear gas in this city as a last resort.

that's the last straw
nun schlägt's dreizehn
That's the last straw, Bruce! I want you to leave this classroom right now. And don't come back until you can behave.

LAUGH

don't make me laugh
daß ich nicht lache
Don't make me laugh, Barbara. Your brother never worked a day in his life. He is the world's laziest man.

laugh something off
etwas auf die leichte Schulter nehmen
Everyone tells him that he should work harder and study more. Otherwise he won't become a doctor. But George just laughs it off.

laugh up one's sleeve
sich ins Fäustchen lachen
You're sad and angry but your neighbour is laughing up his sleeve.

no laughing matter
nicht zum Lachen
Let me tell you that drunken driving is no laughing matter.

die laughing
sich totlachen
They say that he's got a face that only a mother could love. And she died laughing, too.

LEAF

shake like a leaf
wie Espenlaub zittern
Please close the window, Alphonse. It's so cold in here. I'm shaking like a leaf.

die laughing

take a leaf from someone's book
sich jemanden zum Muster nehmen
Neil doesn't drink, doesn't smoke, doesn't stay out late at night. Bill, why don't you take a leaf from his book?

turn over a new leaf
ein neues Leben beginnen
Yes, I'm going to stop drinking and smoking and staying out late at night, Martha. I'm going to turn over a new leaf tomorrow.

LEARN

she has learned her lesson
jetzt weiß sie Bescheid
We all know that Mary has learned her lesson well, because she doesn't play roulette any more.

learn from experience
aus Erfahrung lernen
How do you become a wise man? You become wise by learning from experience. And how do you gain experience? Well, you gain experience by making a lot of mistakes in life.

learn the hard way
Lehrgeld zahlen müssen
I learned that honesty is the best policy the hard way.

LEAVE

take leave of one's senses
den Verstand verlieren
Have you taken leave of your senses, Henry? That's white wine. You don't drink white wine with steak.

leave it at that
es dabei lassen
"Okay," said the policeman, "we're not going to say or do anything more about this matter. We're going to leave it at that."

leave much to be desired
viel zu wünschen übriglassen
"You're a good writer, George," said his agent to him, "but this last story of yours leaves much to be desired."

leave no stone unturned
nichts unversucht lassen
Believe me, Paula. We left no stone unturned but we still couldn't find your purse. I'm afraid it's lost for good.

leave someone in the lurch
jemanden im Stich lassen
He is a true friend and he has never left me in the lurch.

LEG

not have a leg to stand on
keine stichhaltigen Argumente/Beweise haben
"Don't worry, Ernest," said my lawyer to me, "we're going to win this case. The other party doesn't have a leg to stand on."

be on one's last legs
auf dem letzten Loch pfeifen
I'm going to have to stop working soon. I am so tired. I am on my last legs. You'll have to get someone else for tonight.

pull someone's leg
jemanden auf den Arm nehmen
Margaret told me that she had won three million dollars in Las Vegas. I believed her. But then she started smiling and I knew that she was only pulling my leg.

shake a leg
die Beine unter den Arm nehmen
"Come on, Mike. Shake a leg! The taxi's waiting. If we don't hurry, we won't catch our plane on time."

LET

let on that
sich anmerken lassen, daß
Don't let on that you know all about his plans.

let someone down
jemanden im Stich lassen
In all the years I've known Helen, she has never let me down.

let things slide
die Dinge vernachlässigen
Unfortunately, Horst has let things slide at the office.

LIE

a white lie
eine Notlüge
Except for an occasional white lie, he always tells the truth.

lie through one's teeth
das Blaue vom Himmel herunterlügen
Not a word of what you say is true. You're lying through your teeth again. Now, please tell me the truth.

take something lying down
sich etwas gefallen lassen
"Are you going to take what he said to you lying down, Tom?" I asked my good friend. "I certainly am not," he said.

LIFE

not on your life
auf keinen Fall
Do you think he would loan me a hundred dollars? Not on your life!

for the life of me
beim besten Willen
For the life of me I can't remember how it happened or when.

be the life of the party
Leben in die Gesellschaft bringen
Everybody always invites David, because he is the life of the party.

have the time of one's life
sich köstlich amüsieren
All I can say is that I had the time of my life last night at your birthday party, Helen.

LIMELIGHT

be in the limelight
im Rampenlicht stehen
That's the trouble with all politicians. They always want to be in the limelight.

LINE

drop someone a line
jemandem ein paar Zeilen schreiben
If and when you have some time, drop me a line, Jake. I'd like to hear from you. Okay, bye for now.

put everything on the line
alles aufs Spiel setzen
He put everything on the line, including his good reputation.

step out of line
aus der Rolle fallen, aus der Reihe tanzen
If you step out of line here at the academy, we will have to ask you to leave. Is that understood?

toe the line
sich einfügen
If you want to keep your job with our company you will have to toe the line. That's the way the president wants it.

LIVE

live and learn
man lernt nie aus
I didn't know that Christopher Columbus discovered America in 1492. You live and learn.

live and let live
leben und leben lassen
"There will always be people in this world who will be different from you and think differently, too," my mother used to say to me. "That's why live and let live is a good philosophy."

live beyond one's means
über seine Verhältnisse leben
It's no wonder that Mike and Olga have no money. They have lived beyond their means for too long.

LOAF

half a loaf is better than none
ein Sperling in der Hand ist besser als eine Taube auf dem Dach
"This job pays poorly. I earned much more at my last job," I said to my wife. But then she said, "Be glad that you have a job. Half a loaf is better than none."

LOGGERHEAD

be at loggerheads
sich in den Haaren liegen
They're always fighting and having arguments with each other. I guess they're at loggerheads all the time because the both of them are strong personalities.

LOOK

look before you leap
erst wäge, dann wage
It was a big mistake to take that job with that company. I know that now. "Next time," my wife said to me, "look before you leap."

look here!
na, hören Sie mal!
"Look here, James," I said to my neighbour, "I don't want you talking to my children like that. Do you understand?"

look out!
Achtung! Vorsicht! Aufpassen!
"Look out, everyone! Here comes trouble."

look up
sich bessern, sich machen
Business was slow last year. But this year things have started to look up. So business looks good and we are all happy here.

look out for oneself
auf seinen eigenen Vorteil bedacht sein
He is an egoist through and through. The number one rule in his life is to look out for yourself.

LOVE

love at first sight
Liebe auf den ersten Blick
With Christine and Michael it was love at first sight. But with the vampire it was love at first bite.

love is blind
Liebe macht blind
They say that love is blind. But after a while you can see again.

live on love alone
von Luft und Liebe leben
Stanley would love to marry Nancy. He doesn't have a job, money, a house. He would be happy to live on love alone. But Nancy would like to have a little more than that.

love is blind

LUCK

as luck would have it
wie es das Schicksal wollte
We wanted to surprise him in the office, but as luck would have it he
saw us coming and there was no surprise.

just my luck!
mein gewöhnliches Pech!
I had an important job interview yesterday morning. I was running
late. I wanted to take my car but it was a cold winter morning and it
wouldn't start. Just my luck!

be down on one's luck
vom Glück verlassen sein
"Don't feel bad, Ernest," my good friend said to me. "Everyone is
down on his luck sometimes in his life."

have bad luck
Pech/Unglück haben
"If it weren't for bad luck, I don't think I would have any luck at all," said the pessimist.

have more luck than brains
mehr Glück als Verstand haben
When I hear stories about the way Deborah drives a car, well, all I can say is that that girl has more luck than brains.

M

MAKE

make a fuss
viel Aufhebens machen
He's always making a fuss over little, unimportant things.

make a pass at someone
eine Liebelei mit jemandem beginnen
He tried to make a pass at Sylvia at the party last night but he wasn't her type. She wasn't interested.

make believe
phantasieren
It was a rainy day. The small children were unhappy. "Okay," said their mother, "let's make believe it's a sunny day and we're all at the beach swimming and having fun. Okay?"

make do
sich mit etwas begnügen
I didn't have a screwdriver to fix the toaster. I had to make do with a small coin.

make it
es schaffen
I caught my plane in time, but for a while I thought I wasn't going to make it.

make up a story
eine Geschichte erfinden
You better make up a good story why you didn't do your homework if you don't want to get into trouble with the teacher.

MAN

man of letters
Schriftsteller
One day he is going to grow up and be a great man of letters.

man of the hour
Held des Tages
"And now, ladies and gentlemen," said the TV reporter, "here he is. Mr. James Rubinger, man of the hour. The man who saved three children from the flames of that burning house."

man of the world
ein Mann von Welt
Ernest has been to London, New York, Paris, Rome, Berlin, Oslo, Moscow, Warsaw, Madrid. He is really a man of the world.

I'm your man
Sie sind an der richtigen Adresse
Yesterday my boss said that he was looking for someone who would be willing to go to Africa for six weeks on company business. He didn't have the time himself. When I heard him say that, I said, "I'm your man!" I leave for Africa next week.

MARK

make one's mark
sich einen Namen machen
Frank has made his mark in the singing world.

mark my words
denken Sie an meine Worte
"Mark my words," I said to my neighbour. "You'll be sorry that you ever moved into this neighbourhood."

mark time
eine Gelegenheit abwarten
John is just marking time until his boss leaves the company.

MATTER

matter of course
eine Selbstverständlichkeit
It was a matter of course for Ernest to pay the bill when he went out drinking and dining with his friends.

as a matter of fact
in der Tat, tatsächlich
Martina didn't have anything to drink at the party last night. And as a matter of fact, she doesn't drink alcohol at all.

be another matter
ein Kapitel für sich sein
"I know that he smokes 50 cigarettes a day. But I didn't know that he had a drinking problem, Jane." "Yes, he does. But that's another matter. We can talk about it some other time."

MEAN

means to an end
Mittel zum Zweck
It's not a career. It's just a job. It pays the rent and pays for the food. It's just a means to an end.

by all means
aber sicher! selbstverständlich!
Do you mind if I help myself to one of these sandwiches? By all means!

mean business
es ernst meinen
My wife said to me that she would leave me if I didn't stop drinking. This time I know that she means business.

you don't really mean that
das ist doch wohl nicht Ihr Ernst
"Mr. Scanlan," said the boss, "we don't know how we are going to get along without you. But on Monday morning we are going to try. In other words, you are fired." "You don't really mean that!" "But I do, Mr. Scanlan. I do."

MEDICINE

give someone a dose of his own medicine
Gleiches mit Gleichem vergelten
Sandra gave George a dose of his own medicine by saying that she was busy this Saturday night. She was going out with Harry.

take one's medicine
in den sauren Apfel beißen
When I made that big mistake I knew that I would lose my job. I didn't say anything. I just took my medicine and the next day I started looking for another job.

MERRY

the more the merrier
je mehr desto besser
We were having a party. A friend called and asked whether he could bring over ten people. "The more the merrier," I said.

make merry
sich vergnügen
Friday afternoon when work is over we all make merry by going to a nice bar for a few drinks.

MILL

be through the mill
viel durchmachen
Nothing surprises me where women are concerned, because I've been through the mill this past year.

MIND

out of sight, out of mind
aus den Augen, aus dem Sinn
No, I don't remember her. I guess it's true what they say when you don't see a person for a long while: out of sight, out of mind.

be out of one's mind
nicht bei Verstand sein, verrückt sein
He must be out of his mind. We can't pay him that much money.

have an open mind
unvoreingenommen sein
Please try to have an open mind about our daughter's boyfriend.

have a one-track mind
nur einen Gedanken im Kopf haben
Glenn has a one-track mind: money, money, and more money.

know one's own mind
wissen, was man will
The trouble with Stanley it that he doesn't know his own mind.

make up one's mind
sich entscheiden
Have you made up your mind yet? Yes, I have. I'll take this ring.

put something out of one's mind
sich etwas aus dem Kopf schlagen
We are not going to the Bahamas this year, Harry. So, put that idea out of your mind. We're going to Florida this year.

take a load off someone's mind
jemandem einen Stein vom Herzen nehmen
He took a load off my mind when he said that he had found my wallet with all the money and papers still in it.

never mind
es macht nichts
"I'm sorry, George. I forgot to bring your book." "Never mind, Janet. You can bring it tomorrow."

mind one's own business
sich um die eigenen Angelegenheiten kümmern
I wish that he would go away and leave me alone. I just can't understand why some people don't mind their own business.

mind one's p's and q's
nicht aus der Rolle fallen, umsichtig sein
When the president of the company came to inspect the plant, the workers all minded their p's and q's.

MISS

miss someone
jemanden vermissen
I only miss her when I think of her.

135

miss the point
nicht richtig verstehen
"You miss the point, Louis. We don't want you working on this project any longer. We have a better man for the job."

hit or miss
aufs Geratewohl
I forgot which book I hid my money in. So, I started looking in all of them hit or miss.

MONEY

for love or money
nicht für Geld und gute Worte
I wouldn't go back to work there for love or money.

for my money
für meine Begriffe
For my money he is the best computer specialist in the city.

money is no object
Geld spielt keine Rolle
"I'd love to have that coat in the window, dear. But it costs so much money." "If you want it, we'll get it. Money is no object."

money isn't everything
Geld allein macht nicht glücklich
It's true that money isn't everything. There are always credit cards.

be rolling in money
Geld wie Heu haben, steinreich sein
Someday I'll be rolling in money, too.

MOON

once in a blue moon
alle Jubeljahre
Ernest drinks a glass of champagne maybe once in a blue moon.

reach for the moon
nach den Sternen greifen
He thought that you and I would never get together. He thought that I was reaching for the moon. But here we are – together.

reach for the moon

MOUNTAIN

make a mountain out of a molehill
aus einer Mücke einen Elefanten machen
"Look, Olga, all I did was break a glass. It wasn't a vase from the Ming dynasty. So please don't go making a mountain out of a molehill."

move mountains
Berge versetzen
The Chinese say that people who move mountains start by carrying away little stones.

N

NAIL

be a nail in someone's coffin
ein Nagel zu jemandes Sarg sein
I guess you already know that every cigarette you smoke is like a nail in your coffin, Henry.

fight tooth and nail
mit aller Kraft kämpfen
The bank robber fought tooth and nail to get away from the police. But the police were stronger.

hit the nail on the head
den Nagel auf den Kopf treffen
You hit the nail on the head yesterday, James, when you said that it was the lack of ideas from management that was causing this company's financial troubles.

NAME

call someone names
jemanden beschimpfen
They can call me all the names they want to. I don't care. Names can
never hurt me. It just goes to show that I was right.

have not a penny to one's name
keinen einzigen Pfennig haben
George lost all his money in Las Vegas at the roulette tables last week.
And now he doesn't have a penny to his name.

name the day
den Hochzeitstag festsetzen
My girlfriend hasn't named the day yet, but it will be some time this
summer.

NAP

take a nap
ein Nickerchen machen
At work I always take a short nap after lunch. My boss likes to say:
snap back with a power nap!

catch someone napping
jemanden überrumpeln
Our competition caught us napping and that is why they were able to
make a deal with them for a very large sum.

NECESSITY

necessity is the mother of invention
Not macht erfinderisch
During the last war necessity was truly the mother of invention.

the necessities of life
das Lebensnotwendige
Julia is a philosopher but doesn't know it. She says that anything beyond the necessities of life is luxury.

NECK

be up to one's neck in debt
bis an den Hals in Schulden stecken
Most of my good friends are up to their necks in debt.

break one's neck
sich das Genick brechen, sein Bestes tun
I go out and break my neck for him and he doesn't even say thank you.

give someone a pain in the neck
jemandem ein Greuel sein
Nobody likes to have him around in the office, because he gives everyone a pain in the neck.

stick one's neck out for someone
für jemanden die Hand ins Feuer legen
He is one of my best friends. He has stuck out his neck for me in critical situations a lot of times.

NEEDLE

be on pins and needles
wie auf glühenden Kohlen sitzen
I know that I'm going to be on pins and needles until I find out whether I passed that examination or not.

needle someone
gegen jemanden sticheln
He gets very angry if you needle him too often.

NEWS

no news is good news
keine Nachricht heißt gute Nachricht
"I haven't had a letter from Helen in a long time. I wonder if she's okay." "Don't worry, Ernest. No news is good news."

that's news to me
das ist mir neu
"Did you know that Mike and Olga left for California last week?" "No, I didn't. That's news to me."

NICK

in the nick of time
gerade zur rechten Zeit
The policeman arrived on the scene in the nick of time.

NIGHT

have a night off
einen Abend dienstfrei haben
She works in a hospital as a nurse. Sometimes there is so much work to do that she doesn't even have a night off.

make a night of it
die ganze Nacht durchmachen
When we go to Paris for a one-day visit, my wife and I usually make a night of it out on the town.

have a nightcap
einen Schlummertrunk trinken
I think we'd really better go to sleep now, Henry. I think the both of us have had too many nightcaps.

NO

in no time
im Nu
With this new oven, food can be prepared in no time.

no wonder
kein Wunder
"No wonder you're unhappy, Brigitte. You're living in the past."

refuse to take no for an answer
sich nicht abweisen lassen
He is one of our best door-to-door salesmen, because he always refuses to take no for an answer.

NOSE

be as plain as the nose on your face
sonnenklar sein
She loves you, Ralph. It's as plain as the nose on your face.

cut off one's nose to spite one's face
sich ins eigene Fleisch schneiden
If you quit your job, Frank, because of the argument you had with the boss, you'll just be cutting off your nose to spite your face. You'll only be making matters worse for yourself.

pay through the nose
schwer draufzahlen, blechen müssen
A lot of other buyers wanted that house on the hill. I wanted it and I got it, but I had to pay through the nose to get it.

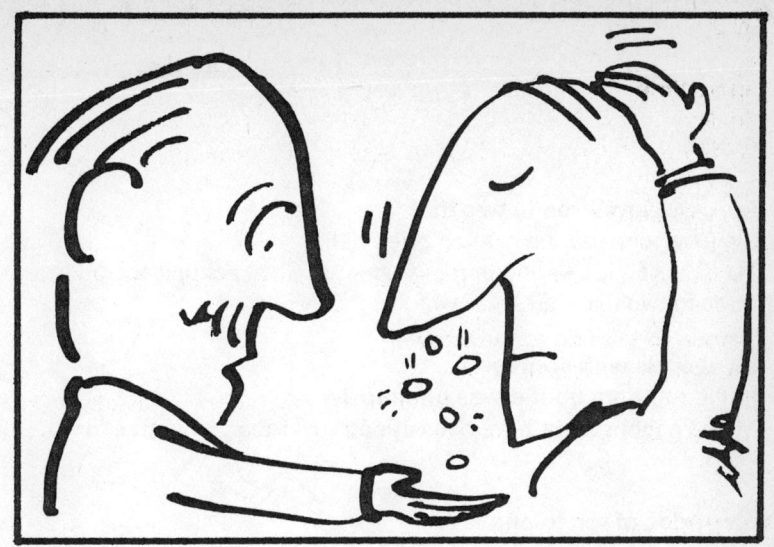

pay through the nose

NOTHING

next to nothing
fast nichts
I paid next to nothing for that car of mine.

nothing doing
nichts zu machen
"Could I borrow your car this evening, Fred?" "Nothing doing. I need it myself tonight."

nothing to write home about
nichts Besonderes
It was a nice film but it's nothing to write home about.

there's nothing to it
es ist nichts dabei
This oven is really simple. You just put in the food and the oven does the rest. Actually, there's nothing to it.

O
_____

ODDS

the odds are three to two that
die Chancen stehen drei zu zwei, daß
My sister Helen knows horses very well. She says that the odds are three to two that that horse will win the race.

be at odds with someone
mit jemandem über etwas uneinig sein
My neighbour and I have been at odds over that apple tree for three years now.

give odds of ten to one
zehn gegen eins wetten
My bookmaker gave me odds of ten to one on a horse by the name of Dolly Silvercloud.

OFF

off and on
hin und wieder, ab und zu
Helen writes to me off and on. I wish she'd write more often.

be a little off
nicht ganz bei Trost sein
Don't mind Linda. She's been a little off these past few days. She has a lot of worries and problems on her mind.

be off duty
keinen Dienst haben
"I can have a glass of wine now," said the policeman. "I'm off duty now."

be well-off
wohlhabend sein
Margaret's uncle left her millions of dollars. So now she is very well-off. But we don't know if she's happy.

have a day off
einen freien Tag haben
I didn't have to work yesterday, because I had a day off.

have an off day
keinen guten Tag haben
George must have had an off day yesterday, because he did practically everything wrong at the office. And he usually is such an excellent worker.

be off-colour
anzüglich sein
Women do not like his jokes because they are off-colour.

OIL

burn the midnight oil
bis tief in die Nacht hinein arbeiten
If you want to be a success in any field, you have to learn how to burn the midnight oil.

pour oil on troubled waters
Öl auf die Wogen gießen
Richard poured oil on troubled waters by sending his editor a small gift. The editor was happy. And everything was okay.

strike oil
einen glücklichen Fund machen
He struck oil when he found out that the people in this small town would just love to have a Mexican restaurant.

OINTMENT

fly in the ointment
ein Haar in der Suppe
It was a great party last night. The only fly in the ointment was Ernest's getting drunk and ruining the fun.

ON

on and on
ununterbrochen
When she starts talking there is no stopping her. She talks on and on.

it's on me
das geht auf meine Rechnung
"Put your money away, Walter," said Ernest. "This dinner is on me."

be on to a good thing
etwas Gutem auf der Spur sein
"I like your idea about opening a Mexican restaurant in this town, Mike," he said. "I think you're on to a good thing there."

ONE

I for one
was mich betrifft, ich für meine Person
"Well, I for one never touch alcohol. I only drink mineral water. That's the only way to stay healthy," Christina said.

be someone's one-and-only
jemandes ein und alles sein
Everyone knows that Christine is Michael's one-and-only.

go someone one better
jemanden überbieten
Our company went them one better: we offered our new clients a three-year guarantee instead of their two-year guarantee.

have one for the road
noch einen zum Abschied trinken
"What do you say, Ernest? Shall we have one more for the road?"
"Yes, let's! One more for my baby and one more for the road."

OPEN

be out in the open
allgemein bekannt sein
The news about what happened here tonight will be out in the open
tomorrow. There were two reporters here at the party tonight.

open up
aus sich herausgehen, auftauen
Most people I know only open up after they've had a few drinks.

OWN

come into one's own
seine Talente zur Geltung bringen
George Scanlan came into his own with his last crime novel.

do something on one's own
etwas aus eigenem Antrieb tun
Martha doesn't have to ask Henry to do the housework when she is at
work in the office. He is a very good husband and does the housework
on his own.

hold one's own
sich behaupten
He will survive in life, because he can hold his own in any situation –
good or bad or difficult.

own up to something
gestehen
The boys owned up to the fact that they had broken the window while
playing ball. The man said it was all right. He had been a boy himself
and the same thing had happened to him, too.

P

PALM

grease someone's palm
jemanden bestechen
We had to grease his palm before he would give us the contract.

have someone in the palm of one's hand
jemanden in der Hand haben
"I've got him where I want him now," John said.
"And where's that?" I asked.
"In the palm of my hand. That's where!"

palm something off on someone
jemandem etwas andrehen
He tried to palm off his personal computer on me saying that it was as good as new. But I knew that it wasn't.

PAT

pat oneself on the back
sich auf die Schulter klopfen
"You can pat yourself on the back, Janice," said the boss. "You really did a good job today, even if I say so myself."

have something down pat
etwas wie am Schnürchen können
I have all the answers that I'm going to give to the police tomorrow down pat.

PIG

buy a pig in a poke
die Katze im Sack kaufen
When you bought that car of yours, Jack, you bought a pig in a poke.

PINCH

in a pinch
zur Not, im Notfall
If you don't have a screwdriver, a small coin will do in a pinch.

be in a pinch
in der Patsche sitzen
You helped me last year, Helen, when I was in a pinch. Now, I'm glad that I can help you.

pinch pennies
jeden Pfennig zweimal umdrehen
I hate it when I have to pinch pennies like this. But there is nothing I can do about it. I hope I'll get a new job soon.

PLAY

call the plays
das Wort führen, das Zepter schwingen
When you're the boss, you can call the plays. But for the time being, I'm the boss. And we're going to do what I say.

play it safe
auf Nummer Sicher gehen
In a situation like this it's always better to play it safe.

a play on words
ein Wortspiel
The following question is a play on words: What is black and white and read (red) all over? A newspaper.

play up to someone
jemanden schmeichelhaft behandeln, jemandem schöntun
She played up to the director of the film because she wanted to get a better part in his new film.

POINT

there is not point in
es hat keinen Zweck zu
All I can say is that there is no point in discussing this matter any further. We aren't getting anywhere with this discussion.

be beside the point
nicht zur Sache gehören
It's nice to know that you had a nice weekend, Frank, but that's beside the point. Today is Monday and we have work to do.

get to the point
zur Sache kommen
It takes him hours to get to the point. He just talks too much.

make one's point
seine Meinung klarmachen
Okay, you've made your point. But I want you to leave now.

up to a point
bis zu einem gewissen Grade
His new book is very good up to a point. And then all of a sudden the quality of the writing drops off.

PRACTICE

practice makes perfect
Übung macht den Meister
They say that Rome wasn't built in a day. And it's the same with anything in this world that takes time to learn. Whether it's a foreign language or the piano: practice makes perfect.

put into practice
in die Tat umsetzen
He is a great talker. But he puts so little of what he talks about into practice.

PRO

weigh the pros and cons
das Für und Wider abwägen
Our company weighed the pros and cons of building a new plant in the United States before it was actually built.

PULL

have pull
Beziehungen haben
My father has pull with that company. Maybe he can get you a job with them. It's worth trying. I'll ask him tonight.

pull oneself together
zusammenreißen
I know that life isn't easy for you right now, Emilio. But try and pull yourself together. Things will get better.

pull one's weight
das Seine tun
"We have a small company here," said the manager, "and that's why I want all of you to pull your weight."

pull the rug out from under someone
jemandem den Boden unter den Füßen wegziehen
My wife and children and I wanted to drive to the mountains last weekend. But the motor in my car was acting up. Well, that pulled the rug out from under us.

pull the rug out from under someone

pull through
durchkommen
"Will he live, doctor?" "Yes, he's going to pull through."

PUT

put it mildly
gelinde gesagt
"I think that Ernest is slowly losing his mind, Barbara." "That's putting it mildly."

put nothing past someone
jemandem alles zutrauen
If my husband came home and said that he had robbed a bank, I wouldn't be surprised. I wouldn't put anything past him when he's drinking.

put oneself in someone's shoes
sich in jemandes Lage versetzen
If you put yourself into his shoes for just a minute, Uli, then you will understand why he acted as he did.

put someone in his place
jemandem eins auf den Kopf geben
It was about time that someone put Bill in his place. And I'm glad that Janet was the one who did it.

put to the test
die Probe aufs Exempel machen
"Do you think this idea of mine will work?" "There's an easy way to find out. Why don't you put it to the test?"

put two and two together
sich seinen Reim auf etwas machen, Schlüsse ziehen
The police knew where the robber was hiding by simply putting two and two together.

put up with something
etwas ertragen, aushalten
She can't put up with his drinking any more. She has decided to leave him for good this time.

Q

QUESTION

leading question
Suggestivfrage
John always asks questions in such a way that you already know what answer he wants. I don't know why he likes to ask all those leading questions.

rhetorical question
rhetorische Frage
Can there be anything better to quench your thirst on a hot summer's day than a glass of cold beer? For a beer drinker that's a rhetorical question.

QUICK

cut someone to the quick
jemanden tief kränken
His unfriendly words and actions cut her to the quick.

as quick as lightning
blitzschnell
Don't think for a minute that he can't move fast just because he's fat. He can be as quick as lightning when he wants to.

quick as a wink
im Nu, im Handumdrehen
The mechanic fixed my automobile quick as a wink.

QUIET

so quiet you could hear a pin drop
so still, daß man eine Nadel fallen hören könnte
When the teacher walked into the classroom all the pupils stopped talking. You could hear a pin drop. It was that quiet.

RACK

go to rack and ruin
zugrunde gehen
That little white house on the island has been slowly going to rack and ruin ever since he moved into it.

put someone on the rack
jemanden auf die Folter spannen
"Tell me, tell me! I have to know. Don't put me on the rack. Did everything turn out all right or not?" I asked Helen.

rack one's brains
sich den Kopf über etwas zerbrechen
For the past week I've been racking my brains thinking how I can come up with some fast money to pay all my bills.

RAG

in rags
in Fetzen
A prince in old clothes that are in rags is still a prince.

go from rags to riches
sich aus der Armut zum Reichtum emporarbeiten
Once he was in America he went from rags to riches in a few short years.

RAIN

rain cats and dogs
in Strömen gießen, Bindfäden regnen
It always rains cats and dogs here in Vancouver in the summer.

when it rains it pours
ein Unglück kommt selten allein
"Oh, Helen. Life has been miserable for me lately. I lost my job, then my wife, then my car, and then my house." "You know what they say, brother dear? When it rains it pours."

rain or shine
bei jedem Wetter
We're going on that picnic tomorrow, rain or shine.

RAT

smell a rat
Lunte riechen, den Braten riechen
We have to stop taking pencils and pens and paper home with us. The boss is starting to smell a rat.

RED

red tape
Amtsschimmel
There is so much red tape that you have to go through before you can start to build a house in this country.

in the red
in den roten Zahlen, verschuldet
Our company has been operating in the red for the past two years.

get out of the red
aus den Verlusten herauskommen
"I'm glad to say," said the company manager, "that this year we are going to get out of the red and make a big profit."

make someone see red
auf jemanden wie ein rotes Tuch wirken
John makes me see red everytime he starts drinking too much wine.

paint the town red
die ganze Stadt auf den Kopf stellen
Last night my wife and I painted the town red.

RIGHT

right away
sofort
I don't want you to do it later. I want you to do it right away, Henry.

be all right
in Ordnung gehen
Don't worry, Ernest, everything is going to be all right.

be on the right track
auf der rechten Bahn sein
The father looked at his son's algebra homework and then said, "Yes, son, you're on the right track."

serve someone right
jemandem recht geschehen
He says he has a bad headache. Well, it serves him right. He stays out late and drinks and smokes too much.

ROAD

be on the road
unterwegs sein
I've been on the road now for more than two weeks.

go on the road
auf Tournee gehen
Our theatre group is going to go on the road next week.

have one for the road
noch einen zum Abschied trinken
We always make it a point to have just one for the road and no more.

hold the road well
eine gute Straßenlage haben
I must say. This car of yours holds the road well.

take to the road
sich auf die Fahrt machen
It was getting late so we decided to take to the road.

have one for the road

ROB

rob Peter to pay Paul
ein Loch aufmachen, um ein anderes zuzustopfen
That's the story of Mike's life. He owes so many people so much money that he constantly has to rob Peter to pay Paul.

ROME

Rome wasn't built in a day
Rom ist nicht an einem Tage erbaut worden
I know that you desperately want to learn to play the piano well. But these things take time, Nicole. You yourself know that Rome wasn't built in a day.

158

do in Rome as the Romans do
mit den Wölfen heulen
I went to a party once where everyone was eating with their fingers.
Well, when in Rome do as the Romans do.

ROSE

see the world through rose-coloured glasses
alles durch eine rosige Brille sehen
I like to have a few glasses of wine sometimes, because I want to see
the world through rose-coloured glasses – even if it's only for a couple
of hours.

ROUGH

be a diamond in the rough
ein ungeschliffener Diamant sein
Give him a little time. He's still a diamond in the rough. With a little
polishing he will sparkle very brightly.

rough it
primitiv im Freien leben
When we spend a weekend in the mountains, we don't even take tents
with us. We really rough it. We sleep under branches.

make a rough copy
einen ersten Entwurf ausarbeiten
Before I started to write this book I made a rough copy first.

RUB

there's the rub
das ist der Haken dabei
"This project is fantastic, wonderful, excellent. The only thing is that
it is going to cost a small fortune."
"Ah, there's the rub."

rub elbows with someone
mit jemandem verkehren
I don't see him that often, but we do rub elbows in Hanover every year during the fair.

rub someone the wrong way
jemandem auf die Nerven gehen
I know that Waltraud is a good person, but she just rubs me the wrong way. And I don't know why.

rub something in
etwas unter die Nase reiben
All right, all right. I know I was in a car accident last week and the car is a complete wreck. But you don't have to rub it in all the time. I said I was sorry, didn't I?

RUN

be on the run
auf der Flucht sein
We were on the run from the police last week. But we didn't do it. They finally caught the men who really did it.

have the run of the place
etwas uneingeschränkt zur Verfügung haben
"I'll be away for about two weeks, Ernest," said the nightclub owner. "While I'm away you can have the run of the place."

run for one's life
um sein Leben rennen
Do you know what that jogger over there is doing? Yes, he's running for his life.

run out on someone
jemanden im Stich lassen
She ran out on me when I needed her the most. Well, that's life.

run someone down
jemanden in den Dreck ziehen, schlechtmachen
I left my wife after ten years of marriage, because she was always running me down. I just couldn't take it anymore.

run through one's mind
jemandem im Kopf herumgehen
"What's running through your mind, Frank?" "Nothing much, really. I was just daydreaming. That's all."

be run-of-the-mill
von Durchschnittsqualität sein
The film that we saw last night was just run-of-the-mill.

S

SAFE

safe and sound
gesund und munter
When the police found the boys they were safe and sound in a small house but cold and hungry.

safe landing
glatte Landung
Our pilot was able to make a safe landing during the snowstorm.

be safe to say that
ruhig sagen, daß
I think that it is safe to say that those people won't be bothering us for a long, long time.

SALT

an old salt
ein alter Seebär
He knows everything about the oceans and the seas and about sailing.
He's been everywhere. He's an old salt.

be not worth one's salt
keinen Schuß Pulver wert sein
If a soldier in the Roman army did not fight well, they used to say that
he was not worth his salt. They used to pay Roman soldiers in salt.

SAVE

save your breath.
sparen Sie Ihren Atem
You might as well save your breath, Mildred. James is not listening to
what you are saying.

save one's skin
mit heiler Haut davonkommen
I was able to save my skin at the last moment by jumping out of the
window. Then the fire swept into the room.

save someone the trouble
jemandem die Mühe ersparen
My husband is such a good man. I was so tired this morning. He saved
me the trouble of making breakfast for the whole family by making it
himself. The children just loved it.

SAY

have a say in something
bei etwas eine Stimme haben
"Listen, Mike," said Olga, "I'm your wife and I have a say in this
important matter, too."

have no say about something
in einer Sache kein Wort mitzureden haben
"You may be my wife, Olga," said Mike, "but you have no say about this important matter at all. That's the way I want it."

have one's say
sich aussprechen
I saw the boss this morning. He let me have my say. And then he kicked me out. Now I can start looking for another job.

be said to be
sollen
They are said to be very rich people but they don't look happy.

as the saying goes
wie man sagt
As the saying goes, Cynthia, a fool and his money are soon parted.

SCRATCH

start from scratch
ganz von vorn anfangen
Throw away those old plans. They're not any good. We know that now. We have to start from scratch, gentlemen.

SECOND

on second thought
bei näherer Überlegung
You know, James, on second thought I'd rather stay at home tonight instead of going out.

be second to no one in
keinem nachstehen in
He is second to no one in the field of computers.

have second thoughts
sich eines Besseren besinnen
I'd like to buy that beautiful car that I saw this morning in town and I told the man I would come in this afternoon, but I've been having second thoughts. It's just too expensive.

SEE

go and see if
nachsehen, ob
Jack, why don't you go and see if there is any mail for me.

see a doctor
einen Arzt konsultieren
I had to go and see a doctor about my arm.

see someone to the door
jemanden hinausbegleiten
Let me see you to the door, Janet.

see things
Gespenster sehen
You should go and see a doctor, Ernest. You're starting to see things. How long have you had this problem anyway?

SELL

be sold a bill of goods
angeschmiert werden
I was really sold a bill of goods when I bought that used car.

sell like hot cakes
wie warme Semmeln weggehen
These new small personal computers are selling like hot cakes.

SHINE

make hay while the sun shines
das Heu ernten, solange die Sonne scheint
You have to work hard now, Christine, while you're still young and
strong. As the saying goes: make hay while the sun shines.

SHOE

if the shoe fits, wear it
sich einen Schuh anziehen, wenn er paßt
The boss isn't saying who always comes too late to work. But if the
shoe fits, wear it.

fill someone's shoes
jemandes Amt übernehmen
Who do you think is going to fill Sandra's shoes now that she's left the
company to go work someplace else?

fill someone's shoes

not want to be in someone's shoes
in jemandes Haut nicht stecken wollen
I wouldn't want to be in Gene's shoes this afternoon when he's there in the boss's office.

put oneself in someone's shoes
sich in jemandes Lage versetzen
If you could only put yourself in his shoes for just a minute, I don't think you would talk about him that way, Glenn.

SHORT

be in short supply
knapp sein
Almost everything is in short supply in that country.

be short of money
knapp bei Kasse sein
John is short of money, you say? Well, what else is new?

cut someone short
jemandem ins Wort fallen
I don't like having a conversation with her, because she is always cutting me short.

make short work of something
kurzen Prozeß mit etwas machen
He made short work of all the reports that he had to write by using a word-processing system.

sell someone short
jemanden unterschätzen
Never sell anyone short just because you think that person is like a mouse. Think of that person as an elephant.

SHOW

stop the show
stürmischen Beifall auslösen
That new singer stopped the show last night on Broadway.

show off
angeben, sich zur Schau stellen
"Look, Ernest," Helen said, "Gene is walking on his hands." "Don't pay any attention to him. He's just showing off."

show promise
verheißungsvoll, vielversprechend sein
"This book is good," said the agent to the author, "but not that good that it could sell. But it shows promise. Work on it a little more. Then come and see me."

show someone around
jemanden herumführen
My brother lives in Paris. He says that when I come to visit him there he is going to show me around.

show someone up
jemanden bloßstellen
You showed him up at the party last night in front of all his friends and family. He didn't like that. Be careful now!

SIGHT

catch sight of someone
jemanden erblicken
If you catch sight of Helen in the crowd somewhere, let me know. I need to talk to her right away.

know someone by sight
jemanden vom Ansehen her kennen
He works here in the company. I don't know what his name is, but I know him by sight.

hate the sight of someone
jemanden nicht ausstehen können
Everybody here in the office hates the sight of the boss.

lose sight of something
etwas aus den Augen verlieren
I think you've lost sight of what you're doing here for us.

not let someone out of one's sight
jemanden nicht aus den Augen lassen
Whatever you do, Henry, don't let the children out of your sight even for a minute.

see the sights
die Sehenswürdigkeiten besichtigen
My brother and I are going to see the sights of Paris today.

buy something sight unseen
die Katze im Sack kaufen
Horst bought that used car sight unseen.

SINK

sink or swim
friß, Vogel, oder stirb
When I lost my job it was a case of sink or swim.

sink in
sich einprägen
I didn't say anything while I was there. I just let his words sink in. I'm going to make a decision tomorrow.

SLIP

give someone the slip
jemandem durch die Lappen gehen
The robber gave the policeman the slip.

slip of the tongue
sich versprechen
I made a slip of the tongue yesterday and everybody laughed.

let something slip by
sich etwas entgehen lassen
You're not going to let this chance of a lifetime slip by, are you, Ernest?

slip one's mind
jemandem entfallen
When I drink too much a lot of things slip my mind.

slip up
einen Fehler machen, sich vertun
We're sorry about the delay, sir. It seems that our head office slipped up a little bit. You'll have the contract tomorrow.

SLY

on the sly
im geheimen, verstohlen
When I was about eleven years old, I used to smoke menthol cigarettes on the sly. That is until my father caught me.

SNAIL

at a snail's pace
im Schneckentempo
When I broke my leg last month I had to walk on crutches. I was a part of the rat race at a snail's pace.

SNAP

be a snap
kein Kinderspiel sein
The language examination was a snap. I was finished in an hour.

snap out of it
eine schlechte Laune überwinden
"Come on, Mike. Snap out of it! It was only a small argument. Your girlfriend will get over it. So, come on, let's smile."

SONG

for a song
für einen Pappenstiel, spottbillig
I bought this dress last week for a song.

SPADE

call a spade a spade
das Kind beim Namen nennen
It's as plain as the nose on your face. Your boss is a gangster. Let's call a spade a spade.

SPEAK

speaking
am Apparat
The telephone rings. George Scanlan answers it. "Hello," he says. The voice on the other end of the line says, "Hello, I'd like to talk to Mr. George Scanlan." "Speaking," says George Scanlan.

speak for itself
für sich sprechen
The good quality and the low price of this product speak for themselves.

speak one's piece
frisch von der Leber weg reden
"You can speak your piece now, George," said the boss. "But when you're finished, I want you to pack your bags, clean up your desk, and then leave the company. You are through."

speak the same language
dieselbe Sprache sprechen
"I don't understand you, Cynthia. And you don't understand me. What else do we have in common besides not speaking the same language?" her boyfriend asked her.

SPICK-AND-SPAN

spick-and-span
blitzblank
When my wife cleans the kitchen it is so spick-and-span that I have to put on my sunglasses. My wife loves that compliment.

SPOIL

spare the rod and spoil the child
die Rute macht aus bösen Kindern gute
My father never hit me as a child. But my mother did. She would always say, "Spare the rod and spoil the child."

be spoiling for a fight
streitlustig sein
"I can tell you're in a bad mood tonight, Frank," said his girlfriend. "You're also spoiling for a fight. Well, you can have a fight if you want one."

spoil children
Kinder verwöhnen
I don't believe in spoiling children too much. Just take a look at what happened to me. My mother spoiled me as a child.

spoil one's appetite
sich den Appetit verderben
If you eat that sandwich now, Ernest, you'll spoil your appetite for the nice dinner that I've made for you.

spoil someone's fun
jemandem den Spaß verderben
Go away! We don't want you around here. You always spoil our fun
with your comments and remarks.

SPOON

be born with a silver spoon in one's mouth
mit einem silbernen Löffel im Mund geboren sein
I have to work for my living. And I have to work very hard for it. I
wasn't born with a silver spoon in my mouth.

STALEMATE

reach a stalemate
an einen toten Punkt gelangen
We had to stop, because the negotiations between our company and
their company had reached a stalemate. As always, it was a question
of money.

STEP

keep in step
nicht aus der Reihe tanzen
You were in the army, Henry. You know what it was like. It's the same
in this company of ours. You have to keep in step if you want to keep
your job.

watch your step
Vorsicht, Stufe!
"Ladies and gentlemen, please watch your step as we go into the next
room," said the museum guide.

step on someone's toes
jemandem auf die Zehen treten
I hope I'm not stepping on your toes when I say that I think you could have written a much better report than this.

STIR

cause a stir
Staub aufwirbeln, Aufsehen erregen
Your negative report about the police in this town caused quite a stir in the mayor's office.

stir up trouble
Unruhe stiften
The mayor doesn't like reporters who tell the truth and stir up a lot of trouble with their newspaper articles.

STOMACH

on an empty stomach
auf nüchternen Magen
I make it a point never to have a drink of alcohol on an empty stomach. Otherwise I would get drunk in no time.

have a cast-iron stomach
einen eisernen Magen haben
Mike can eat absolutely anything, because he is one of those lucky people who have a cast-iron stomach.

lie heavy in one's stomach
jemandem schwer im Magen liegen
The loss of my job lay heavy in my stomach all week long.

turn one's stomach
jemanden anekeln
Just the sight of him turns my stomach.

upset one's stomach
jemandem schlecht bekommen
Drinking too much cola – which I love – upsets my stomach.

STORY

the same old story
die alte Leier
Don't listen to a word he says. He says that he is going to stop drinking, but he never does. It's the same old story all the time.

make a long story short
um es kurz zu machen
"Well, Ernest, to make a long story short: I am in love with you."
"You can make that short story long if you want to," Ernest replied.

SUNDAY

take a month of Sundays
eine Ewigkeit dauern
Don't take your car to that mechanic in town. It takes a month of Sundays before he repairs anything. I really don't know how he stays in business with his slow service.

SURPRISE

be in for a surprise
sein blaues Wunder erleben
Christopher thinks he is going to get the boss's job now that he is leaving the company. But, boy, is Christopher in for a big surprise!

be taken by surprise
überrascht werden
"We were taken by surprise," said the leader of the gang. "Otherwise the police would never have caught us."

come as a surprise
für jemanden unerwartet kommen
"This may come as a surprise to you, sir," I said to my boss, "but I'm leaving the company tomorrow. I quit!"

SUSPENSE

keep someone in suspense
jemanden in Spannung halten
"John, don't keep me in suspense! Did you get the new job or not!" John waited for a minute and then said, "Yes."

SWALLOW

one swallow does not make a summer
eine Schwalbe macht noch keinen Sommer
All right, so he wrote one good book. And it sold a lot. But that doesn't mean anything. Not really. You know what they say? One swallow does not make a summer.

swallow one's anger
seinen Ärger herunterschlucken
I didn't want to lose my job. So, I swallowed my anger and I didn't say anything to my boss.

swallow one's pride
seinen Stolz in die Tasche stecken
I know that you were meant for better things, Richard. But that's the way life is. Just swallow your pride, take the job, and do your work. Something better will come along for sure. In the meantime, we could sure use the money.

swallow the bait
anbeißen
If those buyers swallow the bait, we can make a lot of money by selling this land.

SWING

be in full swing
in vollem Gange sein
"Come in, come in! You're just in time. The party is in full swing."

get into the swing of things
in Schwung kommen
It took the new manager a couple of weeks before he got into the swing of things at the office.

T

TAKE

be able to take a joke
einen Spaß verstehen
The trouble with Harry is that he has no sense of humour. That's why he can't take a joke.

take after someone
jemandem ähneln
Mary's mother is a good writer. And Mary is a good writer, too. Mary takes after her mother where writing talent is concerned.

take a hint
einen Wink verstehen
"Listen, Paul," I said to him, "can't you take a hint? They want you to leave the room for a few minutes."

take care of someone
jemanden betreuen, für jemanden sorgen
His grandchildren took care of him when he was old and grey.

take care of something
etwas erledigen
I'm going to be staying at the office a little bit longer this evening.
There are still a few letters I have to take care of.

take someone's advice
jemandes Rat befolgen
"Take my advice, brother dear," my sister said to me, "and don't
follow anyone's advice. Just do what you think is right."

take something for granted
etwas als selbstverständlich betrachten
If you think he is going to help you in this matter, well, I think you're
wrong. Or at least you are taking a lot for granted. He hasn't helped
anyone this past year.

take steps
Schritte unternehmen
The city took steps to clear the neighbourhood of its slums.

TALK

talk back
frech antworten
He always talks back to all his teachers at school.

talk big
prahlen, angeben
John talks big about how great his book manuscripts are, but he hasn't
sold a single one of them to any publisher.

talk shop
fachsimpeln
Their husbands are computer experts. When the two of them get together at a party all they ever do is talk shop.

talk big

talk something over
etwas besprechen
Before Helen and Gene bought their house in Lathrup Village, they
talked it over for a long time.

talk to oneself
Selbstgespräche führen
My wife once said to me that when I am old and grey I will most likely
be sitting on a park bench and talking to myself.

talk with one's hands
mit den Händen reden
The only way to keep him from talking all evening is to tie his hands
up, because he can only talk with his hands.

178

TEARS

be moved to tears
zu Tränen gerührt sein
She was moved to tears when she heard an old song that reminded her of her husband and herself in happier days.

break into tears
in Tränen ausbrechen
He broke into tears when she told him she didn't love him.

move someone to tears
jemanden zu Tränen rühren
His books are so sad that they move me to tears. But I still love reading them. They are so good and kind and gentle.

shed tears
Tränen vergießen
Why shed tears over something that might have been, Ernest? You know what they say. It's over. Nobody wins.

wipe away one's tears
die Tränen abwischen
When I was a child my mother used to wipe away my tears. But now I am a grown man and I have to wipe them away myself.

TEETH

by the skin of one's teeth
mit knapper Not, mit Hängen und Würgen
We escaped from that burning apartment building last week by the skin of our teeth.

get one's teeth into something
sich in eine Sache verbeißen
When he gets his teeth into some project, there is no stopping him. He will work on it day and night until it's finished. That's just the way he is.

TELL

there is no telling
man kann nicht wissen
You have to be careful when you go out somewhere with John.
There's no telling what he might say or do.

tell on someone
jemanden verpetzen
When we were kids at school we never told on anyone when the teacher asked us who did something.

tell someone off
jemandem gehörig die Meinung sagen
The secretary told the manager off. She was very angry.

TERM

be on good terms with someone
mit jemandem auf gutem Fuß stehen
He and I have been on good terms with each other for a long time now.
And I hope we continue to remain on good terms.

come to terms with someone
sich mit jemandem einigen
It's a small office and I know that that's a problem. But the both of you will have to come to terms with each other if you want to continue working peacefully here in the office.

THICK

be in the thick of things
mittendrin sein
I'm sorry but I can't come now. I'm in the thick of things at the moment. Maybe later, okay?

through thick and thin
durch dick und dünn
We've been through thick and thin together.

lay it on thick
dick auftragen
All right, Henry. We know that you have been having a lot of problems lately. We know all about it. But you don't have to lay it on so thick. We're your friends. We believe you.

THING

be the latest thing
der letzte Schrei sein
This model here is the latest thing in computers, gentlemen!

THROW

throw in the towel
das Handtuch werfen
After working on the project for two years, the architect finally threw in the towel.

throw one's weight around
auf seinen Einfluß pochen
After he had published one book, he started throwing his weight around and telling other young writers how they should write their books if they wanted to get published.

throw up
sich erbrechen, sich übergeben
I was in the jungle. I was very hungry. I ate a few worms that I found on the ground. But then I had to throw up.

THUMB

rule of thumb
Faustregel
A good rule of thumb for drinkers is not to drink on an empty stomach. An even better rule of thumb is not to drink any alcohol until you are at home, safe and sound, sitting in front of the television set.

be all thumbs
zwei linke Hände haben
I'm all thumbs when it comes to repairing anything in the house.

be under someone's thumb
unter jemandes Fuchtel stehen
Poor old Jerry! He's under his wife's thumb all the time.

twiddle one's thumbs
die Daumen drehen
He is such a lazy man. He just sits around all day and twiddles his thumbs.

thumb a ride
per Anhalter fahren
I once thumbed a ride all the way from Detroit to Los Angeles.

thumb one's nose
eine lange Nase machen
Don't thumb your nose at what he says, Bill. He really knows what he's talking about. Just listen and you'll know that I'm right. Please give him a chance.

TONGUE

be on the tip of one's tongue
jemandem auf der Zunge liegen
I know that I know the name of that singer. His name is right on the tip of my tongue. I'll have it in a minute.

bite one's tongue

sich das Lachen verbeißen

The boss called all of us into his office. Then he started to talk. I saw that he was serious. But what he said was so funny that I had to bite my tongue to keep from laughing.

hold one's tongue

den Mund halten, schweigen

"Hold your tongue, Henry," his wife said to him. "I'm the one who's doing the talking here. Not you."

hold one's tongue

tongue in cheek
ironisch gemeint

"I'd like to work for this company for the rest of my life. I'm so happy here," William said. "He just said that tongue in cheek, Martha," his wife said to her friend.

TOOTH

have a sweet tooth
ein Leckermaul sein

I ate three chocolate bars, one piece of cake, and a big bowl of vanilla pudding last night. I really had a sweet tooth last night.

TOP

from top to bottom
von oben bis unten

I searched the house this morning from top to bottom but I still wasn't able to find my ring.

be on top
an der Spitze sein

The only place that I would like to be in this company is on top. There is no other place that I would rather be.

come out on top
als Sieger hervorgehen

It doesn't matter what you had to do to get to where you are now. The main thing is that you came out on top. That's all that really counts in the business world.

stay on top
sich oben halten

As a singer he has stayed on top of the entertainment world for the past twenty years.

TOUCH

get in touch with someone
sich mit jemandem in Verbindung setzen
Jack got in touch with Mary last week to find out whether she would be coming to New York this week as planned.

keep in touch with someone
mit jemandem in Verbindung bleiben
"Let's keep in touch with each other," I said to my good friend. "I'll write if you write. Okay!?" "Okay!"

put the finishing touches on something
die letzte Hand an etwas legen
Before the waiter took out the dinner to the guests in the restaurant, the chef put the finishing touches on the salad.

be touched by something
von etwas gerührt sein
I was touched by the kind words in your letter, Helen.

touch upon
ein Thema berühren
The professor talked mainly about the history of the United States but he did touch upon some other subjects, too, but only very briefly.

TREE

bark up the wrong tree
auf dem Holzweg sein
If you think I'm going to lend you the money to buy that car, then all I can say is that you are barking up the wrong tree.

miss the forest for the trees
den Wald vor lauter Bäumen nicht sehen
The professor had so many problems on his mind to think about that he missed the forest for the trees.

TRIMMINGS

with all the trimmings
mit allem Drum und Dran
Helen made a dinner for her boyfriend with all the trimmings.

TROUBLE

ask for trouble
den Ärger herausfordern
Yes, I heard what those two men at the bar said. But I'm going to stay here. I don't want to go asking for trouble. After all, words can never hurt me. But fists can.

be in trouble
in einer schwierigen Lage sein
I called my good friend Mike and told him I was in a lot of trouble with the police. He is a lawyer and a good one. He said he would help me.

be worth the trouble
der Mühe wert sein
Sometimes I get the feeling that it's just not worth the trouble to help him. He never even says a word of thanks.

give someone trouble
jemandem zu schaffen machen
My back has been giving me a lot of trouble lately.

save someone the trouble
jemandem die Mühe ersparen
Thank you for saving me the trouble of going into town to pick up those books myself, Jack. I appreciate it very much.

TRUE

be true of someone
auf jemanden zutreffen
Frank is big and brave and honest. But that is also true of Thomas.

come true
sich erfüllen, wahr werden
He sent me a card on my birthday and in it he wrote, "I hope that all your dreams come true, Helen."

ring true
echt klingen
I like his short stories because every word rings true.

TUNE

change one's tune
andere Saiten aufziehen
"You come to work late. You drink on the job. You don't do your work as well as you could. You go home early. Now listen, Andrew. If you want to keep your job with this company," my boss said to me, "you are going to have to change your tune. And that means starting as of right now."

U

UNDER

under cover of darkness
im Schutz der Dunkelheit
The two young boys were able to escape from their kidnappers under cover of darkness. Then they notified the police.

under separate cover
mit getrennter Post
My sister wrote me a letter the other day from Detroit, Michigan and said that she was sending me a book under separate cover. She hoped that I would like it. I did.

UP

the ups and downs of life
die Wechselfälle des Lebens
I've seen good days in my life and I've seen bad days, too. Sometimes the days have been better and sometimes worse. That's the way life is. I know all about the ups and downs of life.

be up against something
gegen etwas zu kämpfen haben
The past few days I have been up against a big problem and I still don't know how to solve it. But I know I will.

be up and around
wieder auf den Beinen sein
I was in bed with a cold last week. But I'm up and around again and I've never felt better in my whole life.

be up in the air
unentschieden sein, in der Luft hängen
Plans for building the new factory near the river are still up in the air. They are going to make a decision next week.

be up to no good
nichts Gutes im Schilde führen
I don't know what he's been doing with himself the past week. But one thing I know for sure. He's been up to no good.

move up in the world
in der Welt vorankommen
Last year he bought a new house. Last month he bought himself a big
expensive car. Last week he even bought himself a new fantastic colour television set. He's really been moving up in the world.

speak up
lauter sprechen
Would you please speak up, Sandy. I can hardly hear you.

turn up
auftauchen
I hadn't seen my good friend Mike for ten years. And then one day he
turned up right in front of my house. Just like that.

USE

be of no use
unbrauchbar sein
This typewriter is of no use to me, because it doesn't have the special
keys that I require to type up my report in French.

have little use for someone
für jemanden nichts übrig haben
Our manager has little use for salesmen who do not work hard.

put something to good use
Gebrauch machen von etwas
"Thank you for the money, Mom," I said. "And don't worry. I'll be
able to put it to good use. Once again, many thanks, Mom."

use something up
etwas aufbrauchen
We used up the dishwashing liquid last night. That's why I couldn't
wash the breakfast dishes this morning.

V

VALUE

be of value to someone
jemandem nützlich sein
"Thank you for these books, Mrs. Carruthers," I said to my neighbour, "My brother is a professor at the university and I know that these books will be of value to him."

place a great value on something
großen Wert auf etwas legen
One of the many reasons that I love my husband is that he places a great value on spending a lot of time with our children.

take something at face value
etwas für bare Münze nehmen
My father, whom I loved very much, once told me never to take anything what a politician says at face value.

VARIETY

for a variety of reasons
aus verschiedenen Gründen
When they asked the politician why he didn't keep his election promises, he simply answered, "For a variety of reasons." My father was right. Never trust a politician.

for the sake of variety
zur Abwechslung
I'm going to wear tennis shoes to work today just for the sake of variety. I'm tired of wearing leather shoes.

VENT

give vent to one's feelings
seinen Gefühlen freien Lauf lassen
Sandra always starts to cry when she thinks about the boyfriend that she lost, because she always gives vent to her feelings. If she had them under control, she wouldn't cry so much.

vent one's anger on someone
seinen Zorn an jemandem auslassen
"Don't vent your anger on me, Mark," said the wife to her husband, "just because you lost your job yesterday. I had nothing to do with it."

VENTURE

nothing ventured, nothing gained
nichts gewagt, nichts gewonnen
One of my teachers at school always used to tell us that it was better to have tried and failed than not to have tried at all. And then he'd say, "Nothing ventured, nothing gained."

VERY

from the very beginning
von Anfang an
Mr. Scanlan has been a great help to our company from the very beginning.

on that very day
gerade an dem Tag
"Did it take place on Tuesday?" "Yes, on that very day. Can you imagine such a coincidence?"

the very best
das Allerbeste
We serve only the very best in this restaurant of ours.

the very thought
der Gedanke allein
Just the very thought of her can bring tears to my eyes.

W

WAIT

wait and see
abwarten
"Do you think my sister's new novel is going to sell well?" I asked my wife. "We'll just have to wait and see, won't we?"

wait for someone
auf jemanden warten
He is an old romantic. He says things like, "If it takes forever, I will wait for you, my dear."

wait one's turn
warten, bis man an der Reihe ist
He told me not to push or to shout. There were plenty of copies for everyone. And, he said, if I just waited my turn I would get a copy of his new book, too.

be on the waiting list
vorgemerkt sein
I wanted to buy one of those new computers today, but they didn't have any in the shop. And there were also around 40 people who wanted one. And I wanted one, too. So, I asked them when I could possible get one. And they said that they didn't know, but that they would make sure that I was on the waiting list.

WALK

in all walks of life
in allen Lebensstellungen
It doesn't matter where they live or where they work, people in all walks of life still have to pay income tax.

be walking on air
im siebten Himmel sein
Ever since she said that she would marry him, Henry has been walking on air. And he hasn't come down yet.

walk in one's sleep
schlafwandeln
We lock the door to our uncle's room, because he is old and walks in his sleep at night.

walking papers
Kündigungsschreiben, blauer Brief
It was an unhappy day for John Smith yesterday. His boss gave him his walking papers. What to do? What to do?

WASTE

haste makes waste
Eile mit Weile
If you want to do something when you only have very little time, do it slowly and not quickly. Because if you do it quickly, you'll most likely make a lot of mistakes and get it wrong anyway. You know what they say? Haste makes waste.

go to waste
vergeudet werden
Don't just sit there! Do something! You're a writer. Write a book or a short story! Don't let your writing talent go to waste, Dorothy.

lay waste to something
etwas verwüsten
The invading army lay waste to all the small villages in the country-side. They burned and destroyed everything.

waste time
vertrödeln
He just sits around in the afternoon wasting his time watching television.

WATER

get oneself into hot water
ins Fettnäpfchen treten, sich in die Nesseln setzen
We don't know how Ernest manages to do it, but he does. His one big specialty in life is getting himself into hot water all the time.

hold water
stichhaltig sein
The police are not going to believe your story, because it just won't hold water.

throw cold water on something
einen Dämpfer aufsetzen
My boss threw cold water on my project yesterday by saying that it still needed work and that it wasn't exactly what management wanted.

make someone's eyes water
jemandem die Tränen in die Augen treiben
Your stories, Gene, are like onions: they make my eyes water.

water down the wine
den Wein verdünnen
The Spanish have a saying that wine has two disadvantages. If you water down the wine, you ruin it; if you don't water down the wine, it ruins you.

WAY

by the way
übrigens
"I'm going home now," I said to my secretary. "Oh, by the way. Did you call and tell my wife that I would be home a little bit later than usual?" "Yes, I did, sir."

one way or the other
so oder so
"We'll get them to talk," said the policeman, "one way or the other. We have ways of making them talk."

the only way
die einzige Möglichkeit
The only way that I know of losing weight on a permanent basis is the slow way, the hard way, the old way: eating less.

be well on the way to
auf dem besten Wege sein zu
My friend Mike is well on the way to becoming the best singer in the country.

have one's own way
seinen Kopf durchsetzen, seinen eigenen Willen haben
"I don't see why you always have to have your own way," said the wife to her husband. "Once in a while I'd like to have my own way, too. I'm tired of doing everything that you want."

lead the way
vorangehen
You lead the way and we'll follow you into the castle, Henry.

WHEEL

be a big wheel
ein großes Tier sein
He thinks he's a big wheel around here, but he hasn't found out that squares don't roll.

wheels within wheels
allerlei Verwicklungen
There are only three short words that can describe the mess he is in and why he is in it: wheels within wheels.

WHISPER

whisper sweet nothings
Süßholz raspeln
"He just sat on the couch next to me," one girlfriend was telling another, "and whispered sweet nothings in my ear all evening."

whisper sweet nothings

WHY

the whys and wherefores
das Wie und Warum
"Don't ask me the why and wherefores, John. I don't know. Go and ask the boss," I said. "I'm sure that he can tell you."

WIND

be out of wind
außer Atem sein
I have to lose some weight. I'm much too fat and I know it everytime I walk up a few stairs. I'm out of wind in no time.

break wind
Blähungen haben
The Japanese have a saying that goes something like this: There is no laughter when you break wind alone.

throw caution to the winds
es darauf ankommen lassen
He threw caution to the winds by betting all his money on red at the roulette table. He was lucky. He won.

WIT

be at one's wits' end
mit seinem Latein am Ende sein
I've tried everything and I've said everything. It's like talking to a wall when you talk to him. I'm at my wits' end. I just don't know what to do. And it's awful.

keep one's wits about one
seine fünf Sinne beisammen haben
If you keep your wits about you in this crisis, Mary, everything will be okay. I just know it.

WOLF

a wolf in sheep's clothing
ein Wolf im Schafspelz
Everyone in the office thinks that he is a wolf in sheep's clothing. But I know that it is exactly the other way around: he is really a sheep in wolf's clothing.

cry wolf
blinden Alarm schlagen
We all know about the young boy that cried wolf once too often. The wolf finally ate him.

keep the wolf from the door
sich vorm Verhungern bewahren
My job at the factory isn't much and it doesn't pay much, but at least it keeps the wolf from the door. And that's important to me and my family.

WOOD

be out of the woods
außer Gefahr sein, aus dem Gröbsten heraus sein
Our company is on its way to recovery and stability, but we are not out of the woods yet. We still have a long way to go.

WORD

in other words
mit anderen Worten
After talking for about ten minutes, Jack said to Jill, "In other words, I love you."

one word leads to another
ein Wort gibt das andere
"You know how it is at these parties when people have had that pro-verbial one drink too many? One word leads to another, and what was at the beginning a nice party turns into a major argument," I said.

breathe not a word about something
von etwas kein Sterbenswörtchen sagen
"Whatever you do, Simon," said the manager to me, "don't breathe a word of this plan to anyone. Do you understand me?"

WORK

be at work on a new novel
an einem neuen Roman arbeiten
"George Scanlan is," the agent said, "at work on a new novel. I am sure that his many readers will be glad to hear that."

have one's work cut out for one
ein gutes Stück Arbeit vor sich haben
My daughter says that she wants to become an actress. Well, I told her that she had her work cut out for her.

work both ways
für beide Parteien gelten
If they can do it, then we can do it, too. They're not the only ones in this business that know about these tricks. They are going to find out that these tricks work both ways.

work out
lösen, eine Lösung finden
I once read about a mathematician who spent almost a year working out a very difficult math problem.

work wonders
Wunder wirken
It's truly amazing what talking to a good friend about your problems can do. Very often a talk like that works wonders.

get worked up over something
sich über etwas aufregen
The reason that a lot of people today are unhappy is because they usually get themselves worked up over practically everything.

WORLD

see the world
in der Welt herumkommen
When I was a young man I once saw a poster that said: Join The Navy And See The World. So, I joined the Navy. And what did I see? I didn't see the world. I saw the sea.

think the world of someone
große Stücke auf jemanden halten
"Beate and Barbara," said Horst, "you are my daughters and you know that I think the world of you two."

WORST

if worst comes to worst
schlimmstenfalls
All I can say is that if worst comes to worst, Michaela, you can come and stay with us for a couple of months.

the worst is yet to come
das dicke Ende kommt nach
If you think this is bad, wait until you see what is going to happen tomorrow. All I can say is that the worst is yet to come, Billy.

be prepared for the worst
auf das Schlimmste gefaßt sein
Mary is a woman who always expects the best but is also realistic enough to be prepared for the worst.

get the worst of it
den kürzeren ziehen
We lost a lot of money on that business deal last week. But we were lucky. The other company really got the worst of it.

WOULD-BE

a would-be writer
ein Möchte-gern-Schriftsteller
Paul is just a would-be writer. He hasn't actually written anything but he's always talking about it at cocktail parties.

WRAP

be wrapped up in one's work
in seiner Arbeit völlig aufgehen
He never finds the time to play golf or watch television or take his children to the zoo, because he is so wrapped up in his work. It's a shame, though.

WRONG

get up on the wrong side of bed
mit dem linken Fuß zuerst aufstehen
What's wrong with you this morning, Jack? Did you get up on the wrong side of bed. It looks like it, doesn't it?

say the wrong thing
etwas Unpassendes sagen
You want me to tell you what's wrong with my husband? Well, I'll tell you. Basically, he always says the wrong thing to the wrong people at the wrong time.

Y

YOU

you bet your life
darauf kannst du Gift nehmen
"Will you be at the party tomorrow evening, Henry?" I asked my neighbour.
"You bet your life I will," he replied.

you can say that again
das kannst du laut sagen
"Isn't this the nicest party that we have ever been to, Gene?" Helen asked her husband. "You can say that again!"

you're telling me
wem sagen Sie das
"Victor is such a good dancer," Ruth said. "I could have danced with him all night last night at the party." "You're telling me!"

Z

ZONK

zonk out
sehr schnell einschlafen
You won't zonk out when you start reading *Master Your Idioms*.

The Quick
Idiom Finder

axe
get the axe   15

B

bag
be left holding the bag   15
be nothing but a bag of
    bones   16
have something in the bag   16

ball
play ball   16
be on the ball   17
get the ball rolling   17
have a ball   17
have a lot on the ball   17
keep the ball rolling   17

bark
his bark is worse than his
    bite   17
bark up the wrong tree   17

bat
go to bat for someone   18
without batting an eye   18

bean
not know beans about some-
    thing   18
spill the beans   18

beauty
beauty is only skin deep   18
that's the beauty of it   18

beggar
beggars can't be choosers   19

belt
hit below the belt   19

tighten one's belt   19
belt someone   19

bird
a bird in the hand is worth two in
    the bush   19
a little bird told me   20
kill two birds with one stone   20

bitter
take the bitter with the
    sweet   20

blue
like a bolt out of the blue   20
have the blues   20
sing the blues   20
once in a blue moon   21

boil
boil down to this   21
at the boiling point   21

bone
a bone of contention   22
feel something in one's
    bones   22
have a bone to pick with some-
    one   22
work one's fingers to the bone
    for someone   22

bottom
from the bottom of my heart   22
hit bottom   22
bet one's bottom dollar on
    something   22

bread
know which side one's bread is
    buttered on   23

E

213

They say that if a man runs after money...

... he is money mad. If he keeps it, he is a capitalist. If he spends it, he is a playboy. If he doesn't get it, he is a good-for-nothing. If he doesn't try to get it, he has no ambition. If he gets it without working for it, he is a parasite. And if he gets it after a lifetime of long and hard work, people will call him a fool who never got anything out of life. But you can learn a lot from a fool like that.

Deutsches Register

231

243

Z

rororo Sprachen

Herausgegeben
von
Ludwig Moos

Gunther Bischoff
Speak you English?
Programmierte Übung zum Verlernen
typisch deutscher Englischfehler
(6857)
Managing Manager English
Gekonnt verhandeln lernen durch
Üben an Fallstudien
(7129)
Better times
Programm zum Gebrauch der
englischen Zeiten (7987)

René Bosewitz/Hartmut Breitkreuz
Do up your Phrasals
Fünfhundert Wendungen wichtiger Verben
(8344)

Claire Bretécher/Isabelle Jue/
Nicole Zimmermann
Le Français avec les Frustrés
Ein Comic-Sprachhelfer (8423)

Ahmed Haddedou
Questions Grammaticales de A à Z
Tout ce que vous avez toujours voulu
savoir sur la grammaire sans jamais
oser le demander (8445)

Hans-Georg Heuber/Marie-Thérèse Pignolo
Ne mâche pas tes mots
Nimm kein Blatt vor den Mund!
Französische Redewendungen und
ihre deutschen Pendants (7472)

C 2199/5

Herausgegeben
von
Ludwig Moos

C 2199/5 a

A·N·D·E·R·S·R·E·I·S·E·N

ro ro ro
sachbuch

C 1089/17

A·N·D·E·R·S·R·E·I·S·E·N

REISESACHBÜCHER

Hartwig Bögeholz/Werner Radasewsky
Almanach 88/89
Adressen, Infos & Ideen (7578)

Das FahrradReisebuch
Herausgegeben vom
Fahrrad-Büro Berlin (7513)

Ingrid Backes
Das Frauen Reisebuch (7572)

Isabelle Jue/Nicole Zimmermann
Sprachbuch Frankreich
(7520)

Emer O'Sullivan/Dietmar Rösler
Sprachbuch Großbritannien/Irland
(7564)

Sprachkollektiv Senzaparole
Sprachbuch Italien
(7571)

rororo sachbuch

C 1089/17 b